*"Every groom
should read this."*
– Allan M., Seattle

*"The bow tie instructions
really worked."*
– Tom G., Miami

*"Couldn't have
made it through
the planning
without this book."*
– Glen S., Los Angeles

*"My wife said
it was a perfect
groom – thanks"*
– Kris R., St. Louis

Having

really

# GREAT

time at your wedding, while still being the perfect

# GROOM

to please your bride

# IS

not an easy job.  It's

# MORE

difficult

# THAN

you can imagine

# JUST

to know everything expected of you before

# THE

big day when you finally put on your

# TUX

# THE GROOM'S GUIDE

## Almost Everything
## A Man
## Needs To Know

**by**
**Vicki Mack**

PINALE PRESS

NORTH END

Published by
**Pinale Press**
P.O. Box 293
Palos Verdes Estates, CA 90274

ISBN 0-9645392-2-5

Cover design and photograph by
Vicki Mack and Caryl MacMaster

Thank You


To my David
who is my own Prince Charming,


And to Caryl MacMaster
who has saved me and a thousand
grooms from countless Disasters.


Caryl and I also wish to thank all the brides and grooms who
have been kind enough to let us share their Special Day!


■

# THE GROOM'S GUIDE
## Almost Everything
## A Man
## Needs To Know
by
Vicki Mack

## Table of Contents

# About the Author

Vicki Mack is a professional wedding photographer in Los Angeles, California.

She has taken wedding pictures for Hollywood personalities, politicians, astronauts, an Oscar winner, and several thousand couples, in locations throughout the country, for over twenty years.

Having witnessed almost every known wedding disaster, Vicki decided it was time to share her experiences with future grooms, so they know everything will be perfect when they put on their tux.

■

# INTRODUCTION

You have finally made the BIG decision and found the girl of your dreams to marry. A few years ago, you would have slipped a ring onto her happy finger, and simply spent the months before your wedding basking in the comfortable attention that used to be the man's role.

Well, times have changed, and today's groom wants to be much more involved in all of the planning stages. In fact, your bride probably encourages you to be.

But no one hints that you are about to embark on some of the most dangerous, nerve wracking months of your life, even if you are a professional test pilot.

Why? Because a bride is an unpredictable creature, and the land of wedding planning has a language all its own. You can learn this language. You can use it to feel confident about yourself and your role as the perfect groom.

If you read nothing else in the book, hang in there for the next few pages. You'll learn what your bride is really thinking, and save you both from misunderstandings that could haunt you and your bride for many future anniversaries.

■

# What Is She Thinking?

(Read This Chapter, If Nothing Else)

## Chapter 1

For 25 years I have been a wedding photographer, sharing with couples the planning of their event and their wedding day. I have seen all kinds of weddings - happy, angry, wonderful, disastrous, joyous, and some filled with hurt feelings.

Many of the 'down' moments come about because of a strange phenomenon of which the groom is unaware, both during the planning of the wedding and the day itself. A little knowledge will keep you calm whenever an incident threatens to become a crisis.

Every woman, from the time she was very small, has a plan in her head for her perfect wedding. Today she may be a student or a corporate executive, but she has known since childhood how she wants to walk down the aisle.

It's also true that the attention span of a bride can outlast her groom's on any subject connected with the big event. Add these two facts together and, if the following story, in some form, hasn't appeared in your recent past, it's sure to show up in the near future.

*Nancy and Bob go into a stationery store to pick out their invitations. They start through a stack of thick books, with Nancy avidly examining each page.*

*After the third book, Bob gets bored and stands up to stretch and look around the store. Nancy says, "Bob, come sit down and help me. This is important."*

*Bob does as asked, and helps her look through the other three books. Then Nancy says sweetly, "Which one do you like, dear?"*

*Trouble is brewing. Bob, whose eyes have glazed over two books ago, says "I don't care, pick whatever you like."*

*"No, I really want your opinion," says Nancy.*

*"Okay, I like this one," answers Bob, choosing one he had noticed before they all started looking alike. "How can you even think of that ugly thing instead of this beautiful one with doves and bells," she exclaims.*

*"Actually, I never really cared for doves," he answers innocently. "I can't believe I'm marrying a man who won't even let me have doves!" she shouts as she slams the book and stalks outside to the car.*

*The next day she and her mother go back to the store and choose a dove-less invitation planned to make every-one happy. Bob, who had never in his life given a thought to the question of doves, feels that he is somehow to blame for something.*

This scene, with countless variations, is played out hundreds of times daily across the country.

How to avoid it in your future?

## THE WHOLE PICTURE

Popular psychology books tell us that women view the world differently than men do.

Women see the world, and everything in it, as one huge, whole object, without divisions or separations. The color of a bedspread is connected to the design of the kitchen toaster, which is connected to her hairstyle. Don't ask why - it just is.

Men, on the other hand, tend to compartmentalize. Monday night is for football. A car should be parked in the garage. The right tool for the job.

This difference extends to the concept of time. Women have none. (Just kidding.) They simply expand it, to include everything they want to accomplish. Men will mentally alot a certain time frame for a task. If it isn't finished on time, they will move on to the next job, and reassign the first one to be completed later.

Let's see how this affects your wedding planning. You will want to help, and plan to do your part. Like rent the tuxedos, choose a D.J., hire a limo. Specific assignments, mission accomplished, on to the rest of the world.

For your bride, from now until your wedding day, that event is her world. And in it, each detail of her life is a connected piece of the entire picture, with no tiny part being less important than another.

Your tomboy tennis partner may stop in mid serve, apparently for no reason. She's wondering if the pink skirt on the next court is a good color for her bridesmaids' nail polish. This is IMPORTANT to her. After the wedding, her game will improve.

Your fiancee who is never late to teach her second grade class may show up an hour late for dinner. She stopped at the mall just for takeout food, tried on shoes for the honeymoon, bought "the cutest" placecards. You will once again have warm food once you're married.

## A SOLUTION

Knowing this difference between the sexes is your first key toward sanity. Planning is the second.

■ When she asks for your help on a choice, try to block out a time with her before a scheduled activity, like a movie date with friends. This gives a definite end to the conversation, even if no decision can be reached at that time.

■ You may want to choose certain tasks to be your sole responsiblity. A warning here - no final arrangement should be made without the bride's approval. *(See below - Chapter 1, Her Perfect Dream, for the reasons.)*

■ Develop the art of patience to a new level. Because every detail is as important as every other one, and her anxiety about each one grows as the magic date approaches, she may act quite unlike the girl you planned to marry. So don't tell her not to worry, ask why some small mishap has her in tears, or take on the florist who can't get the right yellow roses. Just be supportive, and look forward to the honeymoon.

## HER PERFECT DREAM

When your bride was a very young child, she probably played 'wedding'. She, or her doll, or her imagination, wore a veil and a beautiful gown, walked down an aisle, waltzed with the prince. Ask her about it. You may hear a charming story.

This is not something to be taken lightly. She may have her heart set on a sunset ceremony in Hawaii or the splendor of a Gothic cathedral, when reality calls for a modest gathering in the local church you both attend.

So what do you do? Tell her to "get real" and face facts? Or use twenty credit cards to take your friends and family to Hawaii and worry about the bills for years to come? Neither. You certainly didn't choose a wife for her lack of intelligence.

She has obviously already taken stock of the available resources and possibilities for the wedding day. She knows just as well as you that your neighborhood church is not the National Cathedral. She wants to marry you, and will do it in a realistic way.

Realistic doesn't have to mean boring. Did you notice the reference to a 'prince'. This is where you come in. Prince Charming. A key word.

When she was small, your bride imagined gazing into the loving eyes of her prince while she returned his affection with her own complete devotion. You are now the lucky man who will see her eyes smiling only at you. Romance. Another key word. The more of it the better, like points scored in a basketball game.

How to gain Romance Points? We'll find out throughout the book, but right now we want to learn what the imaginary wedding day in her childhood was all about, because that cute little girl is still playing and dreaming inside your grown up, beautiful woman.

First, sit down and really talk to your bride about the wedding. Make it fun. Do it over dinner, or in a park, or at sunset, or on a drive. Remember, we're talking about

Romance here.

Find out what her ideal wedding would be, if she could have anything. Don't say it's too expensive or that you won't learn to waltz, just listen. We're on a fact-gathering mission, not actual planning. (If you truly have always wanted to elope, this is not the moment to burst her bubble.)

What this session will do is give you a way to later understand why your superefficient, athletic, businesslike wife-to-be suddenly wants bells and lace everywhere. You will know that it is because her childhood bridal doll was dressed in yards of lace, and she just can't picture a wedding any other way.

By now you are starting to think, "What about me? It's my wedding too." Yes it is, and your wishes deserve equal attention. Think about what you really want on this important day. If she wants the cathedral and you want the park, major compromises are in order. However, the differences are usually much more subtle.

If you really won't wear a pink bow tie or learn to waltz, by all means make these facts known before the planning gets too far. Your bride does value your thoughts, and will take seriously every word you speak about the wedding. So, be diplomatic and, like the man who was granted three wishes, be careful what you ask for.

Your bride and all the other women involved in the wedding planning will happily spend hours and days going over every possible alternative to every detail. Don't spoil their fun. Join in if you wish, or leave it all to them, remembering that a casual remark from you can throw a wrench into all of their careful plans.

■

Since you have obiously read this far, your bride and I thank you and hope you will continue.

The following chapters are not necessarily arranged in order of timing or sequence of events but, rather, of special importance to the groom.

This book is not intended to be a complete guide to planning the entire wedding. It is a series of hints, help and suggestions about those areas where you, the groom, are expected to take charge. The most important or least-often told information will be at the beginning of each chapter.

The stories you read, *identified like this in italics, are real-life incidents which I have truly witnessed.* Only the names are changed, to protect the unfortunate. They are included in the hope that what you learn here will help make your own wedding day be, truly, perfect.

■

# The Tuxedo

## Chapter 2

Your bride has invested countless hours of thought, miles of driving and probably hundreds or even thousands of dollars on her all-important Wedding Dress.

You will be expected to arrive for the ceremony handsomely attired as her matching prince charming. But your outfit will probably be a rental tuxedo which you picked up that morning.

### Danger! Danger!

*Two hours before his wedding, 25 year old Rob - 6'1" tall and 230 pounds, got dressed at the church. As he stepped into his tuxedo pants, he discovered a problem. One leg was hemmed for a man 6' 1", the other for someone 5' 1". The waistband was large enough to allow pulling the pants up to, but not over his hips.*

*Another unlucky groom, Tom, and his ushers each dressed at home and arrived at the church just in time for their photographs. They were wearing pale tan summer suits. One usher (I kid you not) was wearing white boxer shorts emblazoned with bright red butterflies, visible through the pant's fabric. He truly did not do this on purpose.*

In my years of photographing weddings, I have found tuxedos to be the largest source of wedding day panics. The problems can be divided into two categories - fit and assembly.

# TUXEDO FIT

No matter what the tuxedo shop tells you about their tailoring skill, insist that you and your men must try on the completed ensemble at least one day, and preferably two, before the wedding. If the shop says this is not possible, find another store that will agree.

Be firm with your ushers, best man and both fathers. Make sure that they plan time for this into their schedules and stick to it. If you have men from out-of-town, make every effort to arrange their fittings.

If you are a very clothes-conscious man, skip this paragraph. If you are not, plan to take with you for your fitting someone who is. This may be the bride, your father or mother, the bride's mother, or anyone else who is rather insistent and particular. Don't feel foolish or unmanly while this person scrutinizes your outfit and complains that the legs are too loose or the sleeves too short. The fault is not your physique, but the fit of the suit.

Don't feel apologetic or intimidated about making the store re-alter something. They may tell you everything is fine or "This is the fashion". But you are the one who has to feel comfortable and perfectly dressed, and who will be looking at the photos years after the store has forgotten your name.

There are a number of things to look for at your fitting. Take this page with you if necessary, and make copies of the charts for each man in your wedding party.

| JACKET | Right | Wrong |
|---|---|---|
| Shoulder seam - Fits at the corner of your shoulder. | | |
| Shape - Broader at the shoulders than at the waist. | | |
| Width - Comfortable but not too loose. | | |
| Sleeve length - Should remain one-half inch below the wrist bone when elbow is bent. | | |
| Bottom of jacket - Should fall between the tip of the thumb and the tips of the fingers. | | |
| Buttons - Securely sewn. | | |
| Double breasted jacket - Should not pull at the hips. | | |
| PANTS | Right | Wrong |
| Waistband - Pants stay at your waist but remain comfortable. | | |
| Crotch - Not too long or tight. | | |
| Legs - Not too loose or tight in the seat. | | |
| Length - Should just break over the shoe you will be wearing. | | |
| Buttons, buckles, and zippers - Operate properly. | | |

| SHIRT | Right | Wrong |
|---|---|---|
| Collar - Not too loose or tight. | | |
| Fit - Not too loose or tight. | | |
| Sleeve length - One-half to three-fourths of an inch below the jacket cuff when your arm is held down at your side. | | |
| Studs and cuff links - All accounted for and matching. | | |
| Collar - Properly pressed. | | |
| ACCESSORIES | Right | Wrong |
| All present and accounted for. | | |
| Vest, cummerbund, suspenders - Properly adjusted. | | |
| Tie - Correct size, pressed. | | |
| Buttons, buckles, and zippers - Operate properly. | | |
| Shoes, gloves, hat - Check fit and appearance. | | |
| Socks - Not always included. Should match pant color. | | |

When you finish the fitting, assemble all the pieces into the bag provided by the store.

When it is time to pick up the tuxedos for the wedding, everything really should be double checked. This is time-consuming, but I can't tell you how many panics I have seen over a missing tie or shirt studs when the store is a long distance from the church.

And it's not a bad idea to have an extra tie, cummerbund, set of studs, pair of socks, just in case something is missing in spite of your best efforts.

Whoever picks up the tuxedos should have a list of how many suits he will be getting, who they are for, and what all the parts of each suit should be. He should allow himself enough time to thoroughly check that everything is there.

# TUXEDO ASSEMBLY

You are now ready to dress for the wedding. I know, you did this once before in the tuxedo shop, but there are a number of fine points which you may not have noticed.

### Pants

■ There probably are clips on each side of the waistband. These are for changing the tightness of the waist. Hold one-half of the doubled-over elastic and slide the metal clip to tighten or loosen.

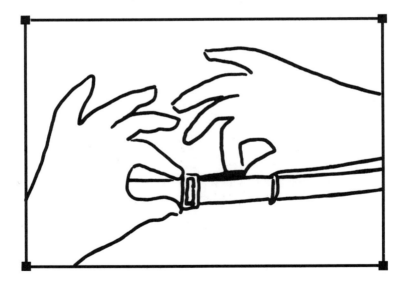

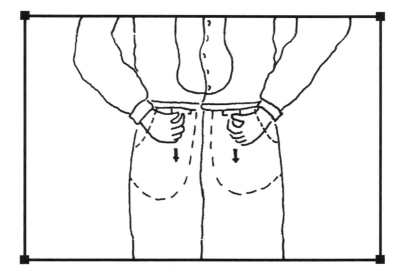

■ If you put your hands into the front pockets and feel along the back of the pocket toward the inside, closest to you, up toward the waistband, you will probably find a slit. This is an ingenious way to keep your starched-front shirt in place. Just reach your fingers through the slit and pull your shirt down whenever necessary. Check this especially during the photographs.

### Shirt

■ See previous page for keeping shirt-front in place.

■ Wing collar points should be tucked under, not above, the tie.

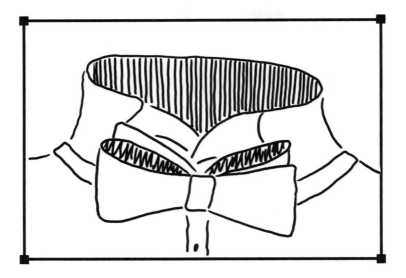

## Cummerbund

■ Pleats should face up, as though you were going to keep change in the folds. If diagonal, they should be from your left to your right.

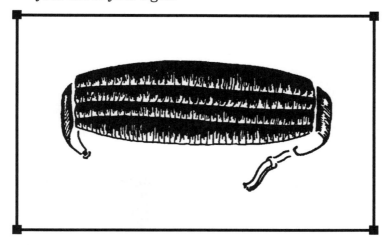

■ The clip in the back can be lengthened or shortened for comfort. See the first point under Tuxedo Assembly/ Pants, page 26.

■ The cummerbund is meant to cover the waistband of the pants. Check during the day to be sure this is where it stays and tighten or loosen the elastic accordingly.

■ White formal suspenders, not black, properly adjusted, will help your pants stay where they belong, around your waist, not your hips.

## Vest

■ Clips at the back of the neck and back of the waist can be adjusted for fit. (See Tuxedo Assembly/Pants, page 22.)

## Tie

■ Clip-on bow ties have a device for tightening or loosening similar to the one on the pants. Adjust so that it looks properly fitted with shirt collar.

■ Ascots should have both ends tucked into vest.

■ A true bow-tie can be tied fairly easily with a little practice. It is not expected to look as perfect and pressed as a clip-on. Many women find them especially sexy, and your bride or any of the women in your family will be happy to help with the tying or untying after they read the following diagram. Have the chosen lady practice before the wedding day, either on you or on her own special man. (Note that the finished product has a loop on one side and a finished end on the other.)

■ Bow ties come in different lengths, and must be the right size for your neck in order to tie properly. Some have an adjustable piece in the back. Check this with your tux shirt on before renting or purchasing a bow tie.

■ The drawing shown on the following two pages is from the point of view of someone else tying your tie. If you are tying it yourself using a mirror, don't forget to look at the drawing in the mirror.

# How To Tie A Perfect Bow Tie

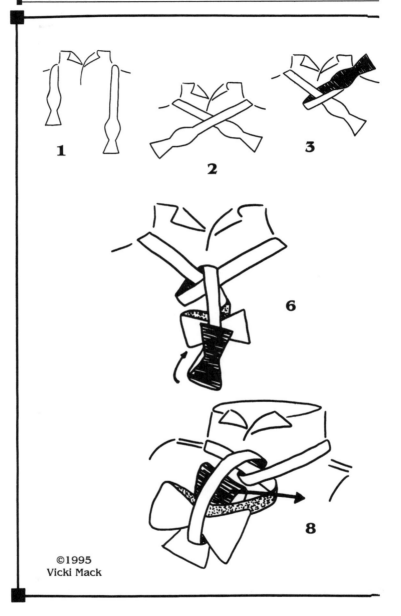

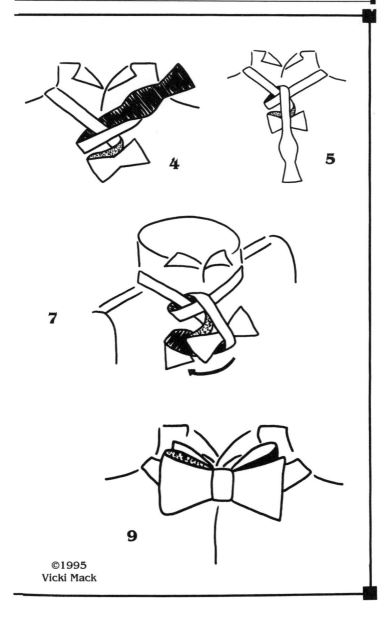

4

5

7

9

# How To Tie A
# Perfect Bow Tie

### Boutonniere

This is the flower worn pinned to the left lapel of all men in the wedding party.

■ Be sure everyone has his in place before photographs begin.

■ Proper placement is in the center of the lapel area below the second point on the left lapel.

■ It is held in place by one or two pins from underneath the lapel, so the pins do not show.

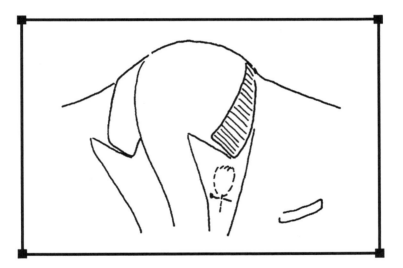

■ Flower is positioned with stem down and flower facing up, the way it would grow. If it is made with a flat side, this goes against the lapel.

## Minor Points

■ Pockets should not contain unsightly bulges from wallets, paperwork, keys, etc.

■ A large sport watch is inappropriate with a tuxedo.

■ Glasses are necessary for seeing, but will cause reflections in your photos. There are two alternatives, short of removing them for your pictures.

A new type of lenses, called non-reflective, work very well but do have a slight blue tint.

You can purchase a pair of frames similar to the ones you normally wear, without lenses. This eliminates the reflection, but may look somewhat unnatural in close-up pictures. Use them only for the photographs, or you could end up married to the wrong girl!

# WHICH STYLE WHEN

Choosing your wedding attire in the first place may sound easy until you enter a tuxedo shop and are faced with a huge array of styles, colors and unfamiliar terms.

Your clothing style is basically influenced by the time of day and formality of your wedding and by the all important style of your bride's Dress. Never forget that, as far as your bride is concerned, her bridal Dress is the most important part of the whole affair, second only to you.

Most tuxedo shops are knowledgeable and helpful at guiding you toward an appropriate outfit for your occasion. If the shop isn't, go find another one. However, to help you enter the store as an informed groom, the next few pages are basic guides to what outfit is correct for what situation.

## FORMAL DAYTIME

| | |
|---|---|
| **Coat:** | Dark grey cutaway. |
| **Pants:** | Striped with pleated or plain front. |
| **Shirt and Tie:** | Starched wing collar shirt with ascot (shown above) or turndown collar with grey and black striped four-in-hand tie. |
| **Vest:** | Pearl grey. |
| **Other:** | Grey gloves, black dress socks, black kid leather shoes. |

## FORMAL EVENING (AFTER 6:00)

| Coat: | Black tailcoat. |
|---|---|
| Pants: | Black. |
| Shirt and Tie: | Starched wing collar shirt with white bow tie. |
| Vest: | White pique (a patterned, heavy white fabric.) |
| Other: | White gloves, black dress socks, black patent leather or kid smooth-toe shoes. |

## SEMI-FORMAL DAYTIME

| | |
|---|---|
| **Coat:** | Black or grey, regular length. |
| **Pants:** | Black and grey striped. |
| **Shirt and Tie:** | Starched turndown collar shirt with four-in-hand grey striped tie. |
| **Vest:** | Dove grey. |
| **Other:** | Grey gloves, black dress socks, black smooth-toe shoes. |
| A dark suit may be used in place of this outfit. | |

| SEMI-FORMAL EVENING (AFTER 6:00) | |
|---|---|
| **Coat:** | **Black tuxedo or dinner jacket. May use white tuxedo or dinner jacket between Memorial Day and Labor Day.** |
| **Pants:** | **Black tuxedo.** |
| **Shirt and Tie:** | **Starched pleated, or soft pique shirt. Black bow tie.** |
| **Other:** | **Black vest, black dress socks, black patent leather or kid shoes. No gloves.** |

| INFORMAL DAYTIME | |
|---|---|
| **Winter:** | Dark suit. |
| **Summer:** | White linen jacket with dark pants, or navy or dark grey jacket with light pants. |
| **Shirt and Tie:** | Starched turndown collar shirt with four-in-hand grey striped tie. |
| **Other:** | Shoes and socks to match pants. |

| INFORMAL EVENING (AFTER 6:00) |
|---|
| Tuxedo or suit, depending on Bride's outfit. Dark suit for winter. Light or dark suit for summer. |

# OTHER CLOTHING STYLES

Changing times bring many other styles which are considered appropriate. They should be carefully considered before choosing them.

*Alan and Sue were married in 1971. He wore the latest style in tuxedos - pale blue with dark blue borders on the wide lapels and on the bell-bottomed pants, and a ruffled shirt with blue trim. He felt very stylish. Now, whenever one of his children's friends look at the photograph hanging proudly in the living room, they giggle.*

Looking at your own wedding photograph ten years from now, your style-of-the-moment outfit may make you feel "dated" or "stylish", depending on your viewpoint.

Modern styles bend the rules of what to wear when. The following are the present-day "conservative" modern outfits.

## CONTEMPORARY
## FORMAL DAYTIME OR EVENING

Black tuxedo, single or double breasted
Black tie and tails
White tie and white tails, white pants (spring or summer)

## SEMI FORMAL DAYTIME OR EVENING

Black grey tuxedo with colored or patterned bow ties
and cummerbunds, often matching bridesmaids' dresses.
Technically, bow ties should not be worn until after 6:00,
however, they are often used with tuxedos for
"modern" daytime weddings.

### Summary of Clothing Choices

Now you know which outfit is appropriate for each time
and type of wedding. But what happens if you want white
tie and black tails, a' la Fred Astaire, your bride sees you in
all white, and your wedding is an informal morning ceremony? In the end, the decision rests with you and your
bride. Your outfit should match hers in style and formality.
Beyond that you can never go wrong by choosing your style
from the charts shown above.

# The Best Man

## Chapter 3

The one choice, other than the bride, which is totally yours, is the best man.

Ushers may be included because they are relatives of yours or hers, because they are related to a bridesmaid, or for countless other reasons. But no one will deny your right to choose the one Best Man, who will stand by you and be responsible for overseeing the duties of the groom's side throughout the day.

Reread that last sentence. It is a definition of the best man. Nowhere does it mention your favorite drinking buddy or even a blood relative, although often one of these men will make a perfect best man.

I can't overemphasize the importance here of the word RESPONSIBLE. As you will see, the best man has to do a lot more than sign the license and hand you the wedding ring at the right time.

So what do you do if your brother or very closest friend is someone who you honestly know is not a good choice for the job? Answer - have two best men, one of whom knows what the job really is all about. This may get you in some hot water with the bride, but explain why it is necessary.

No, she doesn't need two maids-of-honor, although

sometimes this does occur for various reasons. If there is one maid-of-honor, your second (responsible) best man will walk with the bridesmaid next to the maid-of-honor.

The main duty of the best man, which is not stressed often enough, is to stay near the groom throughout the day to help with any situations, from minor to major, which prevent you from being a smooth Prince Charming. You will have a lot on your mind, and shouldn't have to worry about too many details.

Let's break the day into sections, and see how busy the best man really is.

# PRE-CEREMONY

Quite often, the men will put on their tuxedos at the church. The best man should check that all groomsmen are properly dressed, with ties, vests, cummerbunds, etc. put on correctly.

He should do the same with the boutonnieres, making sure they are properly placed and pinned.

During the inevitable men's photo session, he should help keep all of the groomsmen together. There is nothing more frustrating for everyone involved than standing around waiting to take photos because one usher has disappeared to do an errand for his girlfriend.

It is also helpful at this time for the best man to keep an eye on the groom's tuxedo, particularly to see if his shirt is smooth and, with cuffs showing properly, straight for the photos. All photographers may not bother with this, and the pictures will reflect it for years to come.

# B.GOOD
## FOOD WITH ROOTS

B.GOOD
665 Boylston St
Boston, MA 02116

er: Adilson C       07/28/19 4:32 PM
#125          allison Longley

| | |
|---|---|
| Avocado Toast | $3.00 |
| Kale Crush | $6.50 |
| | |
| B.GOOD Rewards Redemption | - $3.00 |
| B.GOOD Rewards Redemption | - $3.50 |

| | |
|---|---|
| Subtotal | $3.00 |
| State Tax | $0.19 |
| Local Ta | $0.03 |
| **Total** | **$3.22** |

| | |
|---|---|
| Credit Card | Swiped |
| Visa | xxxxxxxx1195 |

| | |
|---|---|
| Transaction Type | Sale |
| Authorization | Approved |
| Approval Code | 06135D |
| Payment ID | PFjysPWjJJJR |
| Card Reader | MAGTEK_DYNAMAG |

AVAILABLE REWARDS

Previous Reward Point Balance          5

Next time skip the line - earn points and
redeem or donate rewards. Download our new
app and join B.GOOD Rewards.

Give us your FEEDBACK and we'll give you
$5 off on your next visit!
Feedback.bgood.com

After the photo session, the groom and best man usually go into the pastor's study or some other place away from the arriving guests, so that the groom can make an "appearance" for the ceremony.

This quiet time is a good chance for the best man to recheck preparations for the coming events.

Is the wedding license where it should be? *Tom and Cindy's minister asked their 200 guests to wait for 45 minutes while someone drove home to retrieve the license. He would not perform the ceremony without it.*

Are the wedding rings in place? Sometimes these are both held during the ceremony by the best man, sometimes by the ring bearer, and sometimes one is held by the maid-of-honor. How does the minister want them presented? Will the best man hand them in the box or loose, to the minister or directly to the groom? Will the ring or rings be carried on his finger or in a pocket?

The groom may be nervous at this point as the music begins and guests take their seats. A major job of the best man can be to play psychologist and keep things calm. It is not time to write HELP on the soles of the groom's shoes.

There may be other unexpected last minute duties and errands. The groom may want to say a few words to a parent or friend, who must be found in the crowd and escorted to where the groom is waiting. The groom may have a card or flowers or gift to be delivered to the bride at the last moment. (Good idea - it gives you lots of Romance points with your soon-to-be-wife).

# CEREMONY

Now the time has finally arrived. In most cases, the minister will be the first person to take his position for the ceremony. The next person to appear is the groom, followed by the best man. (An alternative to this is for the groom to be escorted down the aisle by his parents, in which case the best man often enters in the same manner as the ushers).

After the bridesmaids and the bride have walked down the aisle, the best man stands beside the groom for the ceremony. His one duty now is probably, as we have seen, to be in charge of one or both rings.

If the groom has chosen two best men for whatever reason, the ceremonial one, standing next to him, usually produces the rings. *For Dan and Kathys' wedding, this meant that the rings were held by Greg, Dan's 10 year old son, the ceremonial best man. Of course, everyone worried about Greg losing the rings, which he had insisted on carrying around for the hour before the ceremony.*

*When the minister asked for the rings, Greg reached in his pocket and came out empty-handed. He tried the other pants pocket, then his jacket pockets. Everyone held their breath. Still no ring. Finally he went back to the first pocket and produced the ring, turning proudly to the audience to show it off. Everyone laughed and the groom patted Greg's shoulder in relief.*

The entire "act" had been staged by the other, real, best man. In this case, the humor worked, but not every bride or groom, or their parents, would appreciate jokes during what is a solemn moment.

As the ceremony ends, the best man usually escorts the maid-of-honor back up the aisle.

# IMMEDIATELY FOLLOWING
# THE CEREMONY

Now is the time for the best man's other ceremonial duty, signing the marriage license as an official witness.

But other duties are just as important. Before the official wedding party photographs, is the groom covered with lipstick from congratulatory kisses? Is his tuxedo awry from hugs and handshakes? Are all of the ushers present for the photo session, not in the parking lot decorating cars? Does the minister need to be paid - if so, the best man is usually the one who should be prepared with an envelope and the necessary money from the groom.

If the party is leaving the church at this point, are all of the vehicles ready and in place, particularly the car for the bride and groom? If a limousine is being used, is it in place with chauffeur standing by? If champagne has been planned for use in the limo, is it chilled and in place? (This may be another good way to get Romance points with your brand new wife.)

# RECEPTION

Once the wedding party arrives at the reception, the best man can relax, eat, drink and be merry, right? Well, yes, but he also has jobs to perform, so for the sake of the groom, he shouldn't drink too much just yet.

The most noticeable of the jobs is giving the ceremonial first toast. It can be a tricky and trying time for someone unaccustomed to public speaking.

First, the best man should check to see that the liquid

for the toast, often champagne, has been served to everyone. Then, someone must get the attention of the group. This may be the band leader, D.J. or maitre d'. Often, it is the best man himself. He should take his time here.

The finest toast, delivered to a room full of people who have not yet become quiet and attentive, will literally fall on deaf ears.

Remember, this is "show time", and a little showmanship doesn't hurt. If nothing else, tell your best man to slowly count to five before speaking, after he thinks he has everyone's attention. The actual toast is usually written by the best man. Remember, at the beginning of this chapter that I stressed the word responsible? Good topics are short anecdotes of your past friendship, short stories about the bride and groom, what their future plans may be, thanks to the guests for coming, thanks to the parents for providing the celebration, etc.

The best man may, at this time, introduce the wedding party or various relatives by name, if he has been so instructed by the bride and groom.

Topics to be avoided are stories about the groom's old girlfriends, tales of misbehavior by the groom and any long stories which may be funny to a select audience but which can easily bore - or worse, offend - a roomful of people from all types of backgrounds.

As the groom, there is certainly no harm in discussing the toast ahead of time with the best man, especially if you feel that some guidance is necessary.

Until this point in the day, many of the guests, particularly the bride's parents' friends, have not heard you utter a word, other than "I do." The character and personality of the giver of this first toast can be their introduction to what you and your family and friends are really like.

As if all these jobs aren't enough, the best man is technically supposed to escort the maid-of-honor.

This includes, but is not limited to, escorting her to the reception, dancing with her for at least the first official wedding party dance and seeing to her general comfort. If the best man or maid-of-honor plan to have a spouse or date with them, the questions of who sits where and dances when can become complicated. The bride and groom should discuss how they want to handle this. Will the two attendants ride in the bridal car, or with their spouses to the reception? If there is a head table, will it include spouses, or just the actual wedding party? If everyone knows the answers ahead of time, there is less chance of hurt feelings and confusion on the wedding day.

During the rest of the reception, the best man can relax somewhat. He may be responsible for any gifts of money in envelopes given to the groom by guests, or for the groom's going-away outfit, or driving the bride and groom to their hotel, or generally seeing to the groom's welfare.

He may also be the person designated to collect all the tuxedos and return them to the rental shop.

Yes, being the best man is a busy job. It takes thought, patience and planning. You are asking someone you know to spend this festive day thinking mostly about you and your needs, instead of just being a 'party animal'.

You are asking one of your good friends to be just that, a good friend who will stand beside you for the entire day, one of the most important days of your life.

■

# Registering for Gifts

## Chapter 4

Villeroy and Boch. Fitz and Floyd. These are not comedy acts, but potential residents of your new home. They are china manufacturers, and they or their cousins will ship boxes of logo-wrapped merchandise to your bride as gifts from everyone you know.

To the women involved in your wedding planning, the event is one months-long shopping spree. It starts with The Dress and peaks with that frenzy called The Gift Registry.

This is a major raid on one or more specialty or department stores, to select household items, to be purchased by your friends and relatives, which you will look at and use for the rest of your life. It means pondering the merits of Egyptian cotton versus polyester sheets, and wandering through narrow aisles precariously stacked with mountains of expensive glassware. The image of a bull in a china shop may pop into your mind.

Don't even think of joking to your bride, "Hey I've got a good blender, and you've got a whole kitchen full of stuff. What more do we need?" This comment could keep you single for the rest of your life. And saying, "Whatever you choose will be fine with me," may seen like an easy way out of the whole process, but, as you've probably learned by now, she won't be satisfied until you're involved.

Let's first look at the items usually included in the registry, and some of the possibilities. There are huge numbers of gift choices under each heading. The store where you register will have a complete list of selections.

- China - both formal and everyday
- Glassware - fine crystal and everyday
- Flatware - sterling, silverplate and stainless
- Serving Pieces - spoons, bowls, knives, platters
- Small Kitchen Appliances
- Kitchen Utensils
- Linens - bedroom, bathroom, kitchen
- Major Appliances

You'll notice that nowhere on this list is there a category called Tool Chest, or Power Tools, or even one called Camping Gear. (Although Picnic Basket may appear.) If you are foolish enough to mention this omission, the women's reactions can range from a light laugh at your silly joke to fury that you aren't Taking This Seriously.

Before planning a strategy for approaching the registry, let's look at one story to illustrate its importance on your future.

_Scott and two buddies were planning his bachelor party when Veronica breezed into Scott's apartment one afternoon, happily waving a glossy brochure. "Honey, which of these silver patterns do you like the best ?" She set the brochure, slightly dogeared from the months of study by Veronica, on the coffee table in front of him._

_Not wanting to look 'hen-pecked' in front of his friends, Scott picked up the brochure distainfully. "Silverware! What do we need that for?" He tossed the offending literature on the floor, while his friends laughed their agreement._

*Veronica and Scott were married two months later, and didn't register for any flatware at all. Three years went by, and Scott moved up through the ranks of his company, beginning to host business-oriented parties of their own.*

*One night, they were invited to the CEO's house for an elegant dinner. On the drive home, as they savored the rich experience, Scott made the comment. "Did you notice the silverware, Veronica? It was the best I've ever seen. It just felt so good to use, so perfect."*

*Veronica's face flashed fiery red. "That's the silverware I showed you in the brochure. It's terribly expensive. My grandmother wanted to buy us a whole set for a wedding present!"*

Wedding gifts are much more than casual presents exchanged routinely on events like birthdays and Christmas. They are a way for family and friends to bless and enrich the life you and your bride are beginning together. Each item is special to you both as a part of the home you will create, and many of these pieces will probably pass on to a second or third generation. No wonder your bride tries to choose wisely.

## YOUR OVERALL APPROACH

As you have probably already learned from every other wedding detail, your bride has spent hours of thought and poured over pages of ideas for table settings and bedroom designs. When she asks for your opinion, one misplaced comment can undo six months of work. (*See Chapter 1 for general help.*) How are you supposed to know the right answer?

First, remember that your bride carries in her mind the image of her ideal home, even if presently you will be living in a tiny apartment. Each item on the registery list is one puzzle piece in the larger scheme of this perfect picture. Some pieces are more important than others, just as a jigsaw puzzle may radiate out from one or two key cutouts.

China seems to be a bride's most serious selection, with flatware and glasses filling in the boundaries of the picture, and napkins and candlesticks adding those puzzle pieces that aren't really necessary but give the finishing touches. In the bedroom, the bed covering occupies that central spot.

She may never again have the luxury of furnishing your entire home so completely, so let her share this joy with you and with her friends. When those china patterns start looking like so many Frisbees, respect her indecision gracefully and let her rearrange the designs to her heart's content.

*Ryan found the perfect way to approach The Registry, starting with the all-important China.*

*He first asked Donna to show him all of her samples, on one evening when they could spend some time together, for a pre-planned amount of time. He suggested a late Saturday afternoon, when they would have about an hour before going to a birthday party.*

*(Ryan knew his attention span would last that long. Going out together afterward meant he wasn't abandoning her concerns for a football game, while the party turned their conversation to other topics.)*

*After studying her brochures and magazine pages, Ryan realized that he liked the look of dishware with a white* ground (that's the color of the clay), rather than any with an ivory ground. He told this to Donna, adding that its importance to him was about 7 on a scale of 10. So, if an ivory dinner plate was something she absolutely had to have, he could live with it but, given a choice, he preferred the clean lines of white.

Donna, like most brides, took Ryan's words seriously. She thanked him for the help with a kiss, and gathered up her clippings with a purpose, She now had a direction for her search.

Next, Ryan told Donna to pick out three choices for each of the key pieces of the table setting - china, crystal, flatware, accessories. Accompanied by both mothers, they made a visit to the department store where they would register.

Ryan let the three women shuffle the choices this way and that, and listened to all of their comments. By the time they asked for his final vote, he had a pretty good idea of their consensus, and was able to confirm the choices they had already made.

He then took all three happy women to lunch, an activity he had preplanned to once again move forward to life beyond The Registry.

If you follow Ryan's lead, that first sample session can be confusing. Your bride may have eclectic tastes, and will show you designs ranging from formal gold bands to plates decorated with delicate flowers.

Try to find some way to categorize them to suit your own thought patterns, and decide what you think of each category. If you find something you really dislike, alert your bride, <u>nicely, because this may be something she</u>

<u>secretly covets</u>. You'll probably be able to tell by her face. If you see major disappointment, here's a suggestion which will make her smile with the assurance that she's marrying a wonderful man.

Many china patterns have <u>luncheon</u> or <u>salad</u> plates. These are slightly smaller than the dinner size, for obvious reasons. Suggest that, if she really wants this particular sytle, she register for four or six luncheon plates that might <u>mix and match</u> with a plainer pattern, so that she can use them when her friends come for lunch. (Even if your bride is someone who has never hosted a women's luncheon in her life, we're dealing with the ideal home in her mind, remember.)

The same idea can be used in other areas - towels come in guest sizes, even silverware has luncheon and dessert pieces. If these sizes don't exist, repeat the phrase 'mix and match'. It will solve a lot of registry headaches.

You will have solved a problem with compromise, and displayed your understanding and involvement in the whole process.

## TABLEWARE SPECIFICS

### Flatware

More commonly known as 'silverware', this can be the trickiest of the 'big three' to purchase, because looks can be deceiving, especially from a picture. The knife handle that looks so sturdy may really have a lightweight, hollow handle.

Try to find a store where you can hold the forks and spoons to tell how they feel in your hand. Don't feel foolish pretending to cut a steak or scoop up cereal. It's just like trying on a pair of shoes to see if they fit.

Flatware comes in three basic categories, each with pluses and minuses to be considered.

■ Sterling silver - Solid silver all the way through each piece (except knife blades, which are stainless steel), this is the most expensive type, but also the finest. Marked on the back with 'Sterling'.

> Pluses - Will last several lifetimes. Impresses friends and business associates. Makes your wife sparkle whenever she uses it.

> Minuses - Tarnishes constantly. Can be cleaned in a dishwasher, but probably will probably always be done by hand in your home.

■ Silver plate - Silver is electromagnetically plated onto another metal, usually nickel, possibly brass or stainless steel. Comes in a variety of qualities and thicknesses, not easily discernible. Traditionally marked on the back with 'EPNS' or 'Silverplate', but many of the cheaper brands show no marking. Ask questions about quality before buying.

> Pluses - Gives almost the same appearance as sterling without the astronomical price. You will be able to get more of it as presents.

> Minuses - The silver can wear off after repeated polishing. Tarnishes the same as sterling. Is not dishwasher safe, can develop rest spots or peeling.

## DISHWARE

You may have never before noticed the plates set in front of you at every meal, or the designs peeking out from under your mashed potatoes, but your bride certainly has. Once her dress is ordered, she may become obsessed with pages torn from magazines showing china patterns, and will want to draw you into the discussions.

Your bride probably has a pretty accurate mental picture of your future lifestyle and entertaining needs, so following her lead is a good idea. However if your taste varies drastically from hers, there is probably room in your kitchen cabinets to satisfy both. When all else fails, pull out that handy phrase,'mix and match'.

Dishware, commonly known as 'china', or 'plates', can be divided into 'fine china' and 'stoneware'. These terms refer to the type of clay used to make the pieces. Other variations include plastic plates or even paper, but these probably won't concern your bride on her registry list.

■ Fine china - As the name suggests, these dishes are made of very smooth, almost silky clay, and have a layer of extremely smooth decoration and glaze. The better the quality, the less imperfections you will find, such as tiny lumps or pits in the surface. Don't be afraid of fine china. It can stand up to almost anything short of an evening of plate tossing, like Zorba the Greek.

Bone china is considered one of the finest types. It can be quite delicate looking, but isn't as fragile as it may feel in your hands. Real bone is ground up into the clay. This gives the plate added strength and flexibility, while adding a slightly translucent quality.You can impress your bride by knowing how to recognize it. If you hold a bone china plate up to a light, and put your hand behind the plate, you will be able to see the outline of your fingers.

Pluses - Will always be in style. A selection from one of the top companies will insure replacement pieces for many years, in case you have an overwhelming desire to hug your new wife whiles she's washing those expensive dishes.

Minuses - Cost, of course. But, you always get what you pay for. Will probably be lovingly washed by hand, but usually women won't trust a man with this task.

■ Stoneware - Made from a coarser clay, these will be your 'everyday' dishes. Usually thicker than fine china.

Pluses - Less expensive. Dishwasher safe. You won't worry as much about breakage.

Minuses - Patterns change constantly, so broken pieces may not be replaceable. Expect to buy several sets at intervals down the road.

### GLASSWARE

For every beverage invented by man, someone has designed a special glass. Your bride will undoutedly know which shapes are important to her. (For your information, there are even crystal beer glasses!) One basic distinction is important here, loosely defined as 'crystal' and 'everything else'.

■ Crystal, or leaded glass - To make the clearest, most

sparkling glassware, lead is added to the mixture of sand and ask which is melted to make glass. Yes, swallowing lead is toxic, but your drinks aren't in a crystal glass long enough for any lead to leach out.

Recent tests have shown that some decanters have this problem if alcohol is left in them for long periods. If this concerns you, and your grandmother gives you an heirloom piece, pour the wine or brandy into it just before serving, rather than using the decanter for storage.

Designs can be quite thick and pleasantly heavy to hold, or as delicate as a soap bubble. Each piece is blown by an expert, and then the edges are smoothly polished. Stems and bases can be hand made or poured, depending on price. Intricate hand cut designs will be the subject of many of your bride's decisions.

Go with her to the store, and get the feel of various pieces in your hand. Don't be afraid to handle them, they won't drop any easier than the plastic variety.

Find a weight and shape you can both agree on, and let her choose the cut and pattern, unless there's something you hate. Do you really care how many diamond patterns there are on each glass?

■ Everything else - Glass is a very workable medium, and can be rolled, poured, pulled, and pounded, as well as blown by hand or machine. Pick up a tumbler, imagine your morning juice or dinner bevrage in it, try another one. These can be for 'everyday' use or entertaining. Once again quality counts.

## HUNDREDS OF DECISIONS

As an intelligent man, by now you have the general idea. Each item on the registry can have unlimited choices, all waiting to cause a potential crisis in your marriage plans. When that happens, re-read Chapter 1 and recite 'mix and match' several times.

When you get to the store to actually fill out your registry, you may be handed a small scanner, like the one used by grocery store shelf stockers. This does not come with a hip holster like you personal toy six shooter, and should not be fired off blindly at any bar code that dares to cross your path. Whatever you shoot the scanner at will show up a a gaily wrapped package and requires a thank you note.

Your bride is excited about the Registry for two reasons. It combines a favorite sport - shopping - with her version of your life together. Have fun with it and you'll share her enthusiasm for the home you're creating for your future.

■

# The Bride's Dress

## Chapter 5

There will be a presence at your wedding who is just as important to your bride that day as you are, possibly even more so. Your future wife has spent countless hours contemplating, dreaming about, and becoming intimately acquainted with this object, which you have not been allowed to see. It is the star of the show, the all important Wedding Dress.

This Dress has been your bride's partner in her wedding day dreams ever since she was a little girl. You, the groom, are expected to gaze on this white creation with a sincere look of admiring awe as she first approaches you on the aisle. And then, for the rest of the day, she unconsciously hopes you will treat The Dress with the love and respect you usually save for your grandmother or the waxed finish on your new car.

*Karen was a vision of angelic beauty as she floated slowly toward her groom, Carl, on her father's arm, to the regal sound of the church organ. Her dress was shining white silk, as wide at the bottom as the circle for a basketball tip-off. Fabric trailed behind her for the length of an Olympic long jump. Veiling cascaded from her glittering headpiece like a fountain, covering her face and shoulders in the front, stretching down in the back to blanket the white silk train.*

*When the minister finally said, "You may kiss the bride," Carl had no idea how to even reach her.*

_At the reception, the situation was worse. Every time Carl tried to hug Karen, she shrieked loudly as his hand on her back yanked on the veil, which was solidly anchored to her hair. When he tried to follow her, like a good groom, from table to table to visit the guests, he constantly stepped on yards of expensive silk and delicate veil. This earned him scalding looks from Karen for his carelessness, rather than smiling thanks at his patience with her boring great aunt Matilda._

How should you handle the anger you feel that something has, literally, come between you and your bride? By making The Dress your friend and ally, rather than your enemy. This tactic also works well with a new boss or a new auto mechanic.

If you can tell a carburetor from a camshaft, your relationship with your mechanic will be off to a good start. So, to simplify the intricacies of feminine costuming, I give you these diagrams of bridal outfits. (If the rest of this chapter bores you too much, please read the general information under A. The Veil and F. The Train.)

Please note that all pieces are interchangeable with others that clothe the same area of the body.

So, it is theoretically possible to approximate your bride's Dress by tracing over the appropriate pieces and rejoining them. Then, you can learn to correctly handle The Dress, just as you would learn how to change a tire or put down the top on your new convertible.

You need a description of The Dress, which means enlisting the help of the bride or another knowledgeable female. You are risking the bride's wrath here, because she may feel that you seeing The Dress is the ultimate DISASTER. Try to explain to her that you are not risking misfortune or trying to ruin her surprise but, rather, learning how to help her manage her Dress easily on the wedding day.

Hopefully, you will be able to assemble a picture of The Dress before reading the strategies given here, and so will only have to learn about those pieces with which you will come in contact.

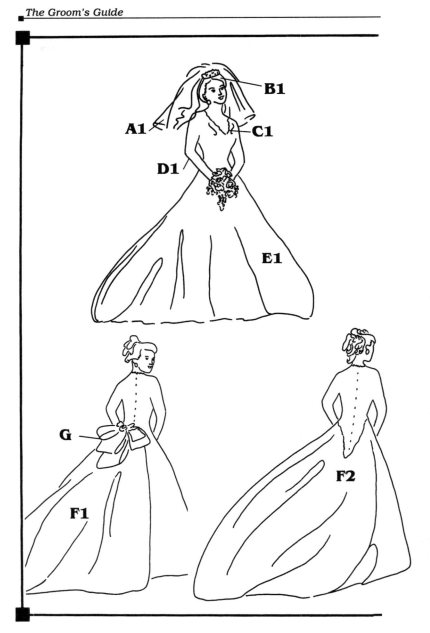

B2

C2

A2

D2

E2

A3

B3

C3
D3

E3

F3

# A. THE VEIL

Most veils are made of a fabric called tulle. It is extremely delicate when your watch band tangles in it, and as tough as iron when it is underneath your hand and being tugged off of your bride's head. If you can find out nothing about The Dress, know that it will probably have a veil.

The absolute worst move you can make all day is, as mentioned above, keep pulling on the fabric when you hug your bride.

SOLUTION - put your hand under the tulle, on her waist or back. This solves the problem and has the added advantage of letting you actually caress your bride rather than a handful of fabric.

The piece of tulle which hangs down in front of the bride's face during the ceremony is called the blusher, not to be confused with the bride's cheekbone makeup, also called blusher.

You will have to deal with the blusher before you can kiss your bride after saying "I do." To do this with style, unrehearsed, in front of everyone you know, is easy when you know how.

Using both hands, held about three feet apart, lightly grasp the tulle at about the level of your bride's chin. (With a long blusher, if you hold it at the bottom, you will find that your arms are not long enough to stretch the tulle back over her head. This leads to all sorts of comedy routines that are not even funny to contemplate when you are the person involved.)

Pull the blusher up and over her headpiece with one sure, steady motion, going as slowly as you like, both for theatrical effect and to make sure that you don't tangle the tulle on any sequins or protrusions of the headpiece.

As you raise the blusher, any tulle which is below your grasp should be folded up so that it can fall down the bride's back gracefully when you have successfully negotiated the headpiece.

Added to this process, remember that your bride is now several inches taller than the girl you proposed to, due to her highest heels and the design of her headpiece. If this makes her uncomfortably tall during the unveiling, hold your hands farther apart, giving yourself enough leeway in the fabric to arch it over her head with the same motion described above.

And, for good measure, gaze directly into your new wife's eyes with all the love you can show, even if you have to glance away long enough to miss the sequined headpiece. Think Rhett Butler as he bent to kiss Scarlett. This look, followed by your kiss, (hand under the veil, remember?), will be rewarded a thousand times in the years ahead, I promise.

## STYLES
*(See Drawing, page 52)*

### (A1) Short veil.
Can be shoulder or fingertip length in back. Comes with or without blusher.

### (A2) Long veil.
May be floor length or trail behind the bride for several yards. Comes with or without blusher. The longest parts may be detachable for the reception. Presents the same problems as the train. (See F. The Train.)

### (A3) Wisp veil.
Very short piece. May float behind the bride or stand almost straight up in waves. Usually has no blusher.

# B. THE HEADPIECE

The headpiece has two functions. First, it gathers the veil together and provides a way to anchor the veil to the bride's head. The attachment usually includes an assortment of bobby pins, all pulling against each other and the bride's hair.

She may not notice any pain until late in the party, when every one of those pins may start to dig into her scalp. If you are lucky, she may stay immune until she changes clothes. Do not suggest removing the veil and headpiece during the reception. It is part of The Dress, and any such suggestion will be considered a criticism of her selection.

The second function of the headpiece is decorative. You probably never have seen your bride wearing a crown, or a large pearl dangling on her forehead, or a hat large enough to sail a catamaran. And you probably will never see her this way again.

But she has spent considerable time in front of mirrors, trying on every headpiece available, to create an effect. A complimentary word will show that you noticed, and it will be appreciated.

In the section on the veil, there is a warning about the headpiece decorations. They can be rhinestones, sequins, pearls on thin plastic strands, a bow, flowers, or the worst, a hat. All of these objects make kissing difficult. However, I have yet to see a groom who couldn't solve this problem, even if your normal style is somewhat curtailed.

### STYLES
*(See Drawing, page 68)*

#### (B1)
Headpiece resting on the top or back of the bride's head. Easiest to anchor in place, hurts the worst when tugged on by the veil.

#### (B2)
Headpiece circling the head and, often, dipping to a point in the front. These are usually anchored only at the back, thus causing the entire front half to lurch upward when the veil is tugged.

#### (B3) A Hat
Comes with or without attached veiling. Guaranteed to inhibit all hugging and kissing of the bride, whether by you or happy friends and relatives. SOLUTION - patience. The hat will come off for the honeymoon.

# C. THE NECKLINE

There is not much to get you in trouble here, although the exact styling is, of course, a feature requiring much study by the bride. Knowledge of your bride's general style will at least make you able to comment intelligently.

## STYLES
_(See Drawing, page 68)_

### (C1) V-shaped or Scooped
Can be moderately or very low cut. Suitable for a necklace given by you as a wedding gift, but check first with someone like her mother to make sure your bride hadn't already planned this Dress to wear with her grandmother's heirloom pearls. If the neckline is extremely low cut, comments like, "How could you wear that in church?" are not appreciated. However, quiet hints to her that her lace underwear is showing at the neckline can be helpful, particularly if you notice this while pictures are being taken. You might also alert a bridesmaid to this fact, and ask her to watch for reoccurrences.

### (C2) High Neck
High neckline. Nothing here to worry about.

### (C3) Wrap
A large wrap of fabric which drapes across both shoulders and wraps all the way around the bride, becoming both sleeve and neckline. (Same as D3) Inhibits upper arm movement. ( Same as D1)

# D. THE SLEEVES
Two problem areas can occur here—your inability to get close to your bride, or her inability to move easily.

## STYLES
_(See Drawing, page 68)_

### (D1) Tight Sleeves
Can be long or short, always tight. She may not be able

to raise her arms very high, for activities like hugging, kissing, dancing, or protecting her hair when the veil is tugged. (Hand underneath at all times.)

### (D2) Puffy Sleeves
Short, puffy sleeve, sometimes with a long, tight piece extending to the wrist. You cannot get close to her without crushing a carefully plumped sleeve resembling a fluffy pillow. SOLUTION - Try to hug or kiss her facing her front, not diving in from the side.

### (D3) Wrap
A large wrap of fabric which drapes across both shoulders and wraps all the way around to bride, becoming both sleeve and neckline. Inhibits upper arm movement same as D1.

# E. THE SKIRT

There are two basic styles here, full and straight. Obviously, the fuller the skirt, the farther you will have to stand from your bride. She did not consider this fact when choosing The Dress. Her only vision was how she would look floating down the aisle toward her adoring Prince Charming.

Please, please, try not to disillusion her. If you treat her, and the Skirt, just the way The Prince treated Cinderella at the ball, she may not know why she is especially happy this day, but you will.

### STYLES
*(See Drawing, page 68)*

### (E1) Hoop Skirt
Not seen too often today, the most difficult to deal with. Has an underlayer consisting of hoops which get larger

toward the bottom. These will only collapse slightly, making sitting difficult, and getting into any vehicle except an open carriage almost impossible.

Positioning your feet too close to her will cause the bottom hoop to tilt sideways, off-balancing the entire skirt, like a bell at the top of its swing. SOLUTION- keep your feet outside of the magic circle, and lean toward her from your waist. Under extreme conditions, you may have to just hold her hand.

Thankfully, these skirts are not seen very often any more, but styles change at any moment.

### (E2) Full Skirt

The most popular style, it can be moderately wide at the bottom or even wider than a hoop skirt. Often held out by one or more layers of crinoline or netting. Difficult to get close to your bride, but not impossible. SOLUTION - move in carefully, parting the waves of fabric so that your feet and legs rest between the folds, the skirt billowing out around your legs.

Remember, when standing side by side it may be more fun to have your hip next to hers, but the best visual effect, for the guests and the pictures, is to lean together closer at the shoulders, leaving room at the hips between you and her for The Dress.

A special category of full skirt looks much like a ballerina, made totally of tulle like the veil. All the above precautions apply, plus the warnings about the delicacy of the veil fabric.

Your watch may catch in her skirt. So will the car door handle, a purse on the back of a chair, part of a flower arrangement. As long as none of this is your fault, try to find a nearby female to disentangle her throughout the day. And, if your watch is the problem, give it to the best man for safe keeping.

### (E3) Straight Skirt

The only problem here is that your bride may not be able to take giant steps, as in (a) going up the altar steps, (b) running out of the church, (c) trying wild dance routines. SOLUTION - (a) Give her your hand and let her take her time. (b) Don't run. (c) Prince Charming dances with Cinderella.

# F. THE TRAIN

Trains are the most annoying part of The Dress, with the veil running a close second. You will first encounter the train, vital to the bride even though you cannot find its purpose, as you exit the church after your ceremony. Here you face one of the groom's worst dilemmas: what to do about the train.

The problem, which will continue all day, is this - she is walking happily along the concrete walkway, when she suddenly remembers that she has, dragging behind her in the dust, five feet of incredibly expensive fabric. She stops. She looks back at her train. She looks imploringly at you.

What do you do? Your first instinct may be to ignore the whole situation. But the helpless look continues. Your next instinct is to step behind her and gather up the offending material. Thousands of manly men before you have done exactly this. However, once you bend down and touch that train, you will be doing it the rest of the day. There is a better way.

This is one of the purposes of bridesmaids. Stop with your bride, look around for one of these girls, show her the problem and politely ask her to carry the train. If no bridesmaids are visible, ask your ever-present and helpful best man to find one or some other nearby female. If all else fails, enlist your best man. At the risk of being labeled antifeminist, I have seen few wedding spectacles sadder than the groom following his bride around with a huge handful of bunched-up fabric.

If no bridesmaid is present when you leave the church, once you arrive at the reception, quietly alert one or more of them that the bride will need help with this problem.

## THE BUSTLE

The train can be permanently hooked up out of the way on many Dresses. It may be gathered up for the reception onto small hooks, so that it becomes merely a part of the skirt. It is then called *the bustle.*

Too often the bustle is still slightly longer than the back of the skirt, causing a trap for the groom if he should step on it and pull the hooks loose. SOLUTION - give the women plenty of time to properly bustle the train, and try to walk ahead of, or beside, your bride at all times.

## DRAPING THE TRAIN

Just because a train is not made to be bustled does not mean it can drag behind the bride on the ground for the day. Someone must carry it. Someone other than you. And you don't want a bridesmaid behind you for the entire reception. Your bride can carry this fabric herself, gracefully, a move she has probably not rehearsed.

You can be her true hero by showing her how to pick up her train, letting the fabric closest to the bottom of her dress hang down behind her arm, draping the middle section of the train over her arm, and letting the pretty lace hem of the train hang down in front. {See illustration below.)

If the train is extremely long, called cathedral length, she can wrap the fabric loosely all the way around her arm before bringing the hem to the front.

### STYLES
*(See Drawing, page 68)*

#### (F1)
Train attached at the back of the bride's waist. May be removable for the reception.

**(F2)**

Train is an integral part of the skirt. Obviously not detachable. May be bustled. SOLUTION- See The Bustle.

**(F3)**

Train attached at the bride's shoulders. If you are lucky, this is removable for the reception. If not, it must be bustled or carried by the bride for the entire day. SOLUTION- See The Bustle or Draping the Train.

# G. THE BOW

A purely decorative accessory which may conceal the hooks for the train's bustle. No problems here.

Now that you are more intimately acquainted with The Dress than you ever wanted to be, let's see how this can help you.

■ You will be able to actually hug your bride without shrieks of pain or anger.

■ You will look like the suave man of her dreams when you lift her veil for the first kiss as husband and wife.

■ You will not spend the day tangled in, crushing, or stepping on your bride's wedding day finery.

■ You will be able to compliment your bride intelligently about The Dress, letting her know how much you appreciate the trouble she has taken to look beautiful for you.

■ You will leave for your honeymoon with a wife who is thrilled with the love shown by her wonderful new husband.

A warning - most tulle is treated with fire retardant solution, but is still dangerous when close to candle flames. During the candle lighting ceremony and the photos after the wedding, help protect the woman you have just married. Don't let her back into a candle - she is several feet wider than she is used to being, and can't see behind her without a rearview mirror, much like a panel truck. She can easily go up in flames when the tulle melts and the glow reaches her flammable hairspray.

■

# The Groom's Men

## Chapter 6

The groom's attendants include the best man, ring bearer, and ushers or groomsmen, who may or may not be the same. (More on that later.)

For now, let's call the combined group the groomsmen. Before going into any etiquette details involving this group, I want to tell you the story of Ken and Alice's wedding.

*They had planned their wedding for months. Many of Alice's relatives, whom Ken had never met, were flying into Los Angeles for the event.*

*The day before the ceremony, Ken's attendants "kidnapped" him for an all-night bachelors' party in Las Vegas. Not wanting to appear to be controlled by his new wife even before the wedding, Ken went along, somewhat reluctantly.*

*They drove two cars for six hours to reach Las Vegas, partied all night (having a great time), and then drove six hours back, arriving just in time for Ken to jump into his tuxedo and get to the church.*

Needless to say, Ken and all his men were slightly hung over and very red-eyed and sleepy. Not exactly the way he or Alice had planned to start married life.

This little tale is only one example of how your fun-loving, well-meaning friends can get confused. Confused? Yes, confused into thinking that something none of them would want done to them 24 hours before, or during, their special day is funny at someone else's wedding.

At the risk of seeming like a 'party-pooper', it's not a bad idea to get this point across to your men. A wedding is a time for fun and togetherness. Of course, bachelor parties are part of this. But they can take place a week before the wedding, to give everyone a chance to recover.

One more thought on this subject, my own pet peeve: drunken groomsmen are not fun. Not for the bride and groom, not for the bridesmaids they escort, not for the guests they greet and seat.

I always shudder when I see an usher with a flask in his pocket before the ceremony, or find all of the men gathered around an ice chest in a car trunk in the church parking lot. These men have a job to do, and stumbling or joking their way through it adds nothing to the dignity and joy of the day.

_Gary's ushers insisted on two rounds of shooters at the reception for all of them, Gary included. Coupled with the champagne and wine Gary had already finished, I leave Gary's condition for the rest of the evening to your imagination and my sympathy to his wife._

Now, assuming your friends would never be guilty of anything like this, let's see what their jobs really are.

# GROOMSMEN

This term, when not used to include everyone, means the men who stand with the groom and best man during the ceremony.

The number of groomsmen is usually planned to match the number of bridesmaids. This often means that your bride will tell you "How many men you can have." Don't fight it - remember, you really did get to pick your best man. Your groomsmen will be dressed the same as the best man. This is often the same as the groom, or there may be a slightly less formal attire for all of your men.

For instance, the groom at a formal wedding may wear white tie and tails. His attendants may wear the same or tuxedos.

### Groomsmen have a relatively easy set of jobs.

- Show up at the scheduled time, properly attired.
- Possibly act as ushers to escort guests to their seats.
- Possibly escort bridesmaids down the aisle.
- Stand with the groom during the ceremony.
- Escort the bridesmaids back up the aisle.
- Stay together and behave for the group photo.
- Possibly escort bridesmaids to the reception.
- Have the first bridal dance with the escorted bridesmaids.

- Other jobs can include decorating cars and any other duties given to them by the groom or best man.

These are your good friends, chosen to be closer to you than the general guests. Hopefully, they will enjoy the honor and have a great time, while becoming instant gentlemen the moment they don their tuxedos.

# USHERS

Technically, these are the men who usher guests to their seats for the ceremony. Often, they are also the same men who stand with the groom and the best man during the ceremony.

Ushers usually need a little briefing on how to do a proper job. As guests enter the church, usually in pairs, an usher offers his right arm to the woman. If he doesn't know the couple, he should ask whether they are friends of the bride or groom, and lead them toward seats on the proper side of the church, with the man following behind the usher and the woman.

Usually the groom's side is on the right as you enter the sanctuary from the back, the brides' side is on the left. In the case of Jewish ceremonies, this is reversed. If the number of guests for each side is very uneven, you may choose to do away with this convention, and seat guests randomly as they arrive.

At most ceremonies, the center aisle is reserved for use by the bridal party. The ushers will use the aisles on each side of the sanctuary to seat the guests.

When women arrive unaccompanied by a man, each should be escorted by an usher. Or, if this is not practical with a group, the usher should give his arm to the eldest and, turning to the others, say "Please follow me." The idea is to seat guests smoothly and efficiently.

A man entering by himself should be escorted by an usher to his seat by simply walking next to him, unless the guest is elderly and needs assistance.

A little light conversation with the escorted guests is nice as the ushers make trips up and down the aisle. If some of your men are young or not very outgoing, give them a few sample ideas - the weather, the decorations, how far the guests have come, etc.

When they are doing duty as ushers only, the men may be dressed the same as the groomsmen or wear something slightly less formal. For instance, if the groomsmen wear tuxedos, the ushers may wear tuxedos or their own dark suits. They do wear a boutonniere, even with a suit, so they can be easily distinguished by the guests.

How many ushers should you have? The rule of thumb is one for every 50 guests, to allow everyone to be seated in a timely manner.

# RING BEARER

A ring bearer can be a tricky thing. Too young, and he can disrupt a ceremony. Too old, and he looks and feels uncomfortable carrying a lacy pillow. Good ones seem to be between ages 3 and 9.

The ring bearer walks down the aisle just before, or with, the flower girl if there is one. If this boy is very young, it is often a good idea to have him walk down the aisle and deliver the rings to the minister or best man and then sit down in a pew during the ceremony. A small bored child climbing around on the altar while you say your vows is very distracting.

Formal attire comes in incredibly small sizes and the ring bearer can be dressed to match the groomsmen or in any number of outfit styles guaranteed to draw comments of "How cute!" from the guests.

A few words on the tricky part of having a very young ring bearer. Sometimes they get stage fright worse than yours, and refuse to go down the aisle.

The best psychology seems to be to station one parent or close friend at each end of the aisle. For instance, Mom at the back of the church with the boy until the last moment, pointing him down the aisle and saying "Walk down there to Daddy." If Mom is a bridesmaid, be sure some other close person is in charge of the boy, who will inevitably start to cry if he is left alone when Mom goes down the aisle without him.

The reason for the ring bearer, obviously, is to deliver the rings. But what if a 3-year-old really changes his mind at the last moment. If there is any doubt, tie fake rings to the pillow and give the real ones to the best man. The show must go on.

If there is one single piece of advice you can have regarding your attendants, it is this: keep them well-informed about what you expect of them, and everyone will have a fun day.

# The Groom's Responsibility

## Chapter 7

Quite easily, someone's feelings can be hurt or a bride reduced to tears because of an oversight by the groom on something for which he did not even know he was responsible.

The worst example of this I have ever seen was at George and Sandra's wedding. *The day had been long and especially hot, with the reception at the bride's parents' home, which was not really large enough for the number of guests.*

*When George finally felt the need to escape with his new wife to quiet and privacy, he took her hand and said, "Let's go. It's time to leave."*

*Sandra's brother, knowing what sticklers for etiquette his parents were, told George that he should thank Sandra's parents before leaving.*

*George wanted to leave NOW. The parents could not quickly be found in the crowd. The brother insisted. George stalked out to his car and sped off, leaving a very unhappy and embarrassed bride behind. George returned an hour later, calmed down and cooled off. I am glad to report that they are still happily married.*

Let's first see what the groom's responsibilities are. This list is one of general wedding etiquette. You and the bride may decide to rearrange or add to this, switching some of the traditional jobs back and forth between yourselves or your families. Usually the groom will:

- Arrange for meetings with your clergyman.
- Choose the best man and groomsmen.
- Obtain the marriage license.
- Arrange for wedding party transportation.
- Provide the guest list from you family's side, with complete addresses and zip codes.
- Plan the rehearsal dinner.
- Choose a gift for your bride, usually presented at the rehearsal dinner or on the wedding day.
- Act like a gentleman throughout the entire event.
- Have a sympathetic shoulder ready when the planning details overwhelm your bride and she needs some extra hugs or someone to run a special errand, even if it's during the big football game.

**What the groom, or his family, traditionally pays for:**
- The bride's engagement and wedding rings.
- The church or clergyman's fee.
- The marriage license.
- The bride's bouquet and going-away corsage.
- A wedding day gift for the bride.
- Corsages for the mothers and grandmothers.
- Gifts for the best man and groomsmen.
- Possibly hotel lodging for out-of-town groomsmen or groom's family members.
- The rehearsal dinner.

- The honeymoon trip is usually added to this list of groom's expenses. Ideally this is nice, because the bride's family is technically paying for the wedding and entire reception.

But I have seen that more often than not, reality is that the bride and groom together have saved for the honeymoon.

It is not uncommon for the groom or his family to help with the total expenses, particularly if the groom has a large number of family and friends. Of course, this is something to be discussed and decided at an early stage in the planning.

The wedding day gift for the bride can be a tricky question. If she has strongly hinted for a string of pearls or earrings to wear with her wedding dress and you can afford them, then you have no problem.

If you have no clue of what to give her or your finances are limited (understandably, with so many expenses), just remember one key word - Romance.

She probably already has your engagement ring, so you don't have to produce the Hope diamond. What you really want to do is bring a tear to her eye and a smile to her heart.

Talk to her mother or best friend for ideas. Jewelry or something you know she wants for your home are almost always safe. A garage-door opener or new garbage disposal doesn't count.

Also remember that presentation is important. This whole occasion is based on fairy-tale time. Some special wine glasses? Tie them to a bottle of champagne. Your grandmother's heirloom ring? Deliver it on a long-stemmed rose. (Be sure someone knows this, so it doesn't get lost.) Whatever you choose, add a note or card, as personal and romantic as you can make it.

Or, if a present really isn't in your plans, make arrangements for someone to deliver your loving note to her sometime before she goes down the aisle.

Now, let's look at the all-important timetable and checklist of what you need to remember. Cut this out if you need to, and put it somewhere conspicuous. Check off various items as you complete them.

### THREE TO SIX MONTHS BEFORE THE WEDDING

☐   Order the bride's rings.
☐   Make out your guest list.
☐   Choose your groomsmen and let them know, particularly if they have to come from out of town.
☐   Choose your wedding attire and decide where you will order it.
☐   Plan with your bride who will really pay for what.
☐   Plan honeymoon with the bride.
☐   Make arrangements for rehearsal dinner.

### ONE MONTH BEFORE THE WEDDING

☐   Be sure all groomsmen go to rental shop for measurements.
☐   Pick up bride's ring and check sizing and accuracy of engraving.
☐   Reconfirm rehearsal dinner plans.
☐   Check with clergyman for any necessary meetings.
☐   Talk to best man about his jobs.
☐   Choose gift for bride.
☐   Choose gifts for groomsmen.
☐   Be sure all transportation is organized, including how you will leave the reception.

## TWO WEEKS BEFORE THE WEDDING

- ☐ Check on all honeymoon plans.
- ☐ Pack for honeymoon.
- ☐ Get travelers checks.
- ☐ Arrange with your bride to go for the marriage license.

Most city halls are rather depressing places, so anything you can do to instill a little Romance is a great idea. Lunch at your favorite restaurant, a bouquet, even a picnic on the courthouse lawn.

- ☐ Prepare your leaving-the-reception outfit.

## ONE WEEK BEFORE THE WEDDING

- ☐ Be sure all groomsmen get tuxedo final fittings.
- ☐ Have your own tuxedo fitting.
- ☐ Remind groomsmen of times they should be at the rehearsal, rehearsal dinner, and church.
- ☐ Give the best man money for the clergyman (in a nice, sealed envelope) and for anyone else necessary.
- ☐ Check with photographer or bride for men's photo time schedule.
- ☐ Be extra, extra nice to your overstressed bride.
- ☐ Have a great bachelor party.

# Service Personnel

## Chapter 8

There are a number of people who help your wedding take place, and care deeply about it, who are neither family nor friends. They are all of the people that are paid to provide a variety of services.

All have their own concerns, and can become your friends or foes. Let's look at things from their perspective and then see how you and they can work together.

## THE PHOTOGRAPHER

I am starting with this person because he is the one you will have the most direct contact with all day. (The fact that this is my profession couldn't possibly have any bearing on this choice.)

My reference to the people producing various services as "he" or "she" is a purely personal choice, depending on which sex I have most often seen performing the particular service.

The photographer, usually a man, has perhaps the most difficult job of the day. He has to pose formal portraits, with all the men's suits perfectly adjusted and the women's gowns perfectly arranged, keeping everyone smiling and looking at the camera at the right instant. And not just once, but twenty to fifty different shots and poses in the shortest possible time, while others are standing behind him, distracting his subjects' attention from his lens. While children are fidgeting, mothers are fussing, the florist is hovering and the bride and groom are trying to be patient.

He must also capture on film every candid moment. This means being in front of the bride and groom with a flash going off in their faces while they return up the aisle, snuggle in their limo, do their first romantic dance, cut the cake and toast each other. And, because not even professional models have their wits about them on their wedding day, he usually must direct them into the most photogenic position for most of these activities. No wonder the groom often wants to punch him.

Then, when the wedding is over, the photographer must produce top quality photos of every single thing. There are no allowable excuses. He can't say "Your brother is missing from the family picture because no one could find him and everyone else was turning nastily impatient," or "There are no pretty pictures of you two in that beautiful garden because the groom threatened physical violence if I bothered him one more time." You get the picture.

So what can you do to ease this tension? It helps to go with your fiance to meet the photographer before she books him for the job, to make sure you have no real personality clashes. You will spend more of your wedding day with the photographer than with anyone else except the bride and your best man.

If you have any particular pictures in mind, or are planning any surprises (a gift to the bride, a spectacular dip at the end of your first dance, etc.) be sure to let him know. A good photographer tries to anticipate the day's actions, but he is not a mind reader. He doesn't know your much-loved great-aunt has flown in from Australia unless you tell him.

If you don't like posing for pictures, tell him, so that he can be extra sensitive to your wishes.

*One of my favorite grooms was Alan, who greeted me and my camera at the church by saying, "I hate having my picture taken, but I promised Alice I would behave, so here I am." I promised to make things as quick and painless as possible, tried to keep him pre-informed as to when he would be needed and for how long, and bothered him only when necessary. We were still friends at the evening's end, when he thanked me for my help.*

Be aware of the camera. Treating it as a friend is a big help to you and to the photographer. He is watching for good candids, especially at the reception. When you do that special dance step, or toast your bride, face the camera if possible. This keeps the photographer from saying "Look over here," or "Do that again" one thousand times during the day. You will want the pictures, and your back is probably not your best side.

One last thing. The photographer has a very long day. He must dress formally, load and check his equipment, and start taking pictures an hour or two before the wedding. He must be cordial and friendly, yet get the job done. He is with you until the bouquet and garter are thrown. Treat him with respect and FEED HIM.

Many photographers are too embarrassed to ask. By the time someone remembers to say "Did you get something to eat?" the food service is finished. If you are serving an elaborate meal on a tight budget, arrange with the caterer to provide sandwiches for him but, if possible, feed the photographer as if he were an invited guest. You will be rewarded with that little extra touch that any person gives when they feel that they matter to you.

# THE VIDEOGRAPHER

Most of the weddings that I photograph now have a professional videographer, which can give you a wonderful memento but doubles the photography problem.

For most of what you need to know to deal with this person, re-read the advice on photographers.

Video equipment does come with its own limitations. There are cables, tripods and lights which may be in the way and patience is in order.

Sound is always tricky. Remember that when a wireless microphone is clipped onto you before the ceremony, everything you say to your best man will be audible on the master tape.

Video cameras do not turn on instantly, even in the standby position. The operator needs to be notified before any activity, so that he can position and turn on the camera to record not just your first dance but also the Master of Ceremonies (M.C.) announcing this event to the guests, and you leading your bride onto the dance floor. Be sure that the M.C. knows this, and be aware of it yourself during the day.

You may forget about the videographer, because he will be shooting behind the still photographer and letting the photographer do all of the directing. Don't forget him at mealtime. FEED HIM, TOO.

# THE COORDINATOR

She is perhaps the most universally disliked person in this chapter.

She may come with the church or be hired for the day and is usually a well-dressed, soft-spoken woman. She may be knowledgeable and tactful, or a grumpy dictator; whichever, no one likes her because her job is to boss everyone around, which is exactly what you are paying her to do.

Her jobs include, but are not limited to, running the wedding rehearsal, making sure everyone is wearing the right flower, showing the ushers how to do their job and making sure they do it, keeping everyone in the right place for the ceremony, quieting the giggling bridesmaids just before the ceremony, and getting everyone down the aisle in the right order.

No one wants to pay attention to her and these details, because they are having too much fun. But when she is not present, there is certainly a greater amount of pre-ceremony confusion and the wedding party then often turns to the photographer to be the coordinator.

To get along with this lady and take some hostility off of your   shoulders, just listen to her.   She is usually a reasonable person, trying to make sure your ceremony goes properly, which is why she is there.

If you do have a coordinator, usually from the church, who acts like a whispering master sergeant dispensing lots of seemingly unnecessary orders, ask her about them. Some of these orders may concern hard and fast church rules, and some may be just the way she has "always done them." Before you argue about them or joke or fume behind her back, find out the reason for any rules that annoy you and then try to negotiate.   Keep in mind that sugar is sweeter than vinegar. Tact, humor and a few compliments will work wonders.

# THE MASTER OF CEREMONIES

This can be the band leader, disc jockey or simply the best man. The style in which he announces the events will set the tone of your reception.

A disc jockey has musical choices ranging from classical to heavy metal, and his personality can vary just as much. So can that of a band leader, although a band doesn't usually have the same range of musical styles.

You have, hopefully, hired your musicians because you like their type of music, so in most cases you can relax and let their leader run the show. If he acts in a way you find distasteful, just tell him.

_Frank and Susan were a sedate couple, as were their friends. Their D.J. apparently thought they were too quiet and tried to liven up the party._

_While Frank and Susan cut the cake, the D.J. loudly urged them to smear the icing all over each other. They wisely refused._

_Susan's very shy friend caught the bouquet, and the D.J. ordered her to sit in a chair in the middle of the dance floor while the young man who caught the garter slid it onto her leg— with his teeth— to the embarrassment of the girl and the guests._

I have seen many weddings where this was done with a lot of fun for everyone, but in this case the D.J. should have been more sensitive to the gathering. And if yours isn't, you are the groom. Don't be afraid to speak up.

Usually, the only complaint with musicians is volume. The band wants to get everyone involved and the simplest way to do this is by turning up the volume so that no one can talk and they might as well dance.

You can tell when the sound is too loud for your guests, even if, personally, your ears love that drum beat. Are the guests sitting silently with glazed-over eyes or leaning over to shout into the ear of their neighbor? Are a lot of people standing in the hallway or next room so they can talk to the people they haven't seen for years?

If so, have the best man ask to have the sound turned down. If this doesn't work, do it yourself, maybe accompanied by your bride. Somehow, her white dress carries more weight here than your tuxedo. Be firm, but not belligerent. You don't want the musicians to pack up and leave, just tone down.

When your M.C. is the best man or a family friend, help make sure he really knows his job: what events he will announce; who will decide on the timing; and what style of M.C. he should be.

If you are planning a short speech (of course you are; see Chapter 11) tell the announcer at the beginning of the reception so that he can put this into the proper spot.

## THE CATERER AND FLORIST

These people are enormously important. They do all of your decorating and feed your guests.

I am not giving them very much space here because usually the groom doesn't have much to do with these people. Details have been taken care of by the bride or her parents and they worry about any glitches.

Your only job here is to be sympathetic to your bride

when minor things go wrong, as they often do. If your bride only has 22 roses in her bouquet instead of the ordered two dozen, or the cake is decorated in emerald green loops instead of pink roses, these are tragedies to her. Don't tell her it doesn't matter, or, when she starts crying at this remark, take out your frustration by asking the caterer how she could be so stupid. Calm your bride with reassurances that everything else looks wonderful, including her. If you feel you must help remedy the situation, ask the appropriate person what, if anything, can be done.

Calmness, reason and humor once again help a lot.

There are countless other people working behind the scenes to give you that perfect day. Limo drivers, groundskeepers and waiters are just a few whom you may or may not even notice.

Each is trying his best to please you. A smile or a "thank you" to any of these people working on your wedding will be appreciated, particularly coming from the groom, who is usually oblivious to all of their efforts. That's part of being a gentleman. It's easy; it comes with the tuxedo.

■

# Limousine Etiquette

## Chapter 9

Most of the weddings that I photograph are in the Los Angeles area. Customs differ throughout the country, but in most places you don't have to be a movie star to hire a limousine for your wedding day. School teachers, construction workers and bankers all feel like stars when they sit back in the plush seats.

## HIRING THE CAR

Transportation is usually included in the groom's responsibilities. If you have hired a limo before and were happy with the company, this is an easy job. If you have not done this, ask your friends for recommendations, or use the telephone Yellow Pages.

When interviewing various companies, ask detailed questions. The chart on the next page is useful for tracking each company's answers.

| QUESTIONS TO ASK EACH LIMO COMPANY | Company: Phone: | Company: Phone: | Company: Phone: | Company: Phone: | Company: Phone: |
|---|---|---|---|---|---|
| What is the hourly rate? | | | | | |
| Minimum number of hours? | | | | | |
| When do charges start and end? | | | | | |
| Is hourly rate discounted over a certain number of hours? | | | | | |
| If the ceremony runs late, are there extra charges? Or will the driver go to another job? | | | | | |
| What about tax and tip? | | | | | |
| Make, model and color of limo? | | | | | |
| What is the seat configuration? | | | | | |
| Will the driver know the route without directions? | | | | | |
| Is there a stocked bar? Does it cost extra? | | | | | |
| Will there be ice and glasses? | | | | | |
| Use check, cash, or credit card? | | | | | |

After completing the interviews, go over the information with your bride.

Most companies have a minimum time charge. This can start when the car arrives or when it leaves the garage to start the job.

Sometimes one consideration will out weigh others. *Mary had her heart set on a white stretch Lincoln. The only one available was $5 an hour more than other cars, but it was worth it to her.*

Decide with your bride where the limo will be used. It can pick her up at her house and stay with you until you reach your bridal suite that night, or it can simply take you from the church to the reception.

Remember that if you have the limo come to the church instead of the bride's house, the bride must plan to get to the church another way. If her father has a large four-door car, this is no problem. But no bride wants to cram her expensive dress into a small car before she walks down the aisle.

*Margaret and her bridesmaids rode to the church standing up in a van, but this is not recommended.*

With planning and some negotiating, you can probably have the car pick up the bride and stay until you arrive at the reception for a reasonable cost.

If your budget is large enough, you may want to hire more than one car. Extra cars can be used for the wedding party and the parents.

*Tina and John were married on the day of the USC-UCLA football game. John's father, a loyal USC fan, hired a limo* with a television set so that, when he was not needed, he could watch the game. This is only recommended if the women in your family are very understanding.

When you have chosen a limo company, ask for a contract which specifies answers to your questions and notes the date, time and place for the car's arrival. Many companies will say that arrangements by phone are all that is needed. Don't believe them.

_That is why Sue and George sat at the church after their wedding for almost an hour while their guests waited at the reception. She did not want to leave without the limo she had already paid for, which had the wrong arrival time scheduled._

# THE DRIVER

When you rent a limousine, you get more than a long car. You get a driver. Usually it is a man and usually he is friendly and helpful.

He should be prepared to perform several functions. They include opening the car door, helping the bride in and out, opening champagne and, most important, piloting the car from place to place without direction from you. Surely you have better things to do in the back seat.

The driver also can be called upon to take someone on last minute errands. Once the bride is at the church, the car and driver are normally idle until you go to the reception, but you are still paying for them.

So, if your mother runs her nylons or someone needs a sewing kit for a repair, you can always send them to the store in the limo. A good driver will help calm jangled nerves and turn such minor crises into a fun excursion.

# USING THE LIMO

Nothing makes you feel quite as elegant as riding in a limousine. Floating down the road behind darkly tinted glass is guaranteed to make anyone feel special. Enjoy it to the fullest.

If you want to decorate the car with flowers, take into account its extra length. If you are having the maid of honor and best man ride with you, make sure the car has seating for four in the back area. If you want beverages in the car, alcoholic or not, plan ahead, including ice. The drinks are probably going to sit in the car all of the time you are in the church.

*Sally and Jim left the church laughing in a shower of rice and stepped into their limo. Sally's smile faded, replaced by a look of disappointment that was very evident to Jim.*

*What was wrong? What had he done? There was no champagne in the empty silver bucket provided with the car. To her, toasting each other in the elegant car would have been romantic and exciting.*

*She had not mentioned this to him, but somehow felt that it was his fault that it was not there. Such is the logical reasoning of a girl about her wedding.*

When you and your bride enter the car, you should first help her in on the side nearest the curb. A bridesmaid or even your best man should handle her large skirt and train. Be sure the door does not close on her dress. Then go around to the other side of the car and use the street-side door to enter. This way the bride does not have to slide that mountain of fabric across the seat.

Most couples will say good-bye to their limo driver when they arrive at the reception, rather than paying for the driver to do nothing during the reception. Just don't forget to arrange transportation for leaving the party.

# OTHER ALTERNATIVES

A limousine is not the only transportation choice other than the family car.

I have seen couples leave their church or reception by boat, motorcycle (watch out for trailing trains and veils), horse, helicopter, balloon, horse and carriage, surfboards and skis. A rented luxury car can be driven by the best man or a friend, for a very reasonable price.

*Todd decided to surprise Helen with a novel way to leave the church. As they came out, their transportation pulled up in front. It was a pedicab piloted by a strong-legged young man in top hat, tails and black shorts.*

*Everyone laughed, but Helen kept looking longingly at the white limousine she had hired, which was parked at the curb.*

*Helen gamely bundled her dress into the pedicab, while the bridesmaids and groomsmen happily climbed into her limo. They made a very slow parade for the four miles to the reception on a very hot day. Helen, Todd and their driver arrived hot and sweaty. The wedding party had a great time.*

This was a cute idea gone bad. Two blocks from the church, Helen and Todd should have probably joined their friends in the limo, but hindsight is wonderful.

One big alternative to a limousine is (don't laugh) a bus. *Susan and Joe had a wedding ceremony in the San Fernando Valley, about 30 miles from their reception at the beach.*

*They were concerned about their guests driving that far to get home after drinking at the reception, so they hired a Greyhound bus to make the trip. They rode on the bus too, and everyone had a great time.*

If there is a lesson to be learned from this section on alternatives to limousines, it is to think and plan carefully. Other choices may be good or bad, but I have never heard a bride complain about having to ride in a limousine.

# The Rehearsal Dinner

## Chapter 10

By now, I can take a pretty good guess at what you've been thinking.

*I just wish she would wear one of those cute dresses that remind me how I love her, and that I could wear my jeans and favorite sweat shirt, and we could simply have a small party with only our family and really close friends.*

Well, surprise, you get to have your wish as part of the wedding. (Everything, that is, except the jeans and sweat shirt. Those may be negotiable, but don't count on it.) We're talking about the rehearsal dinner.

Usually, there will be a practice run-through of your ceremony one or two days before the Main Event. It is held wherever the ceremony will take place, and is directed by the minister or wedding coordinator. Afterwards, there is a dinner for the participants, which serves several purposes.

It will assure everyone involved that they will know their roles in the formal event. It will blend your crazy boyhood chums, your bride's studious best friend, your kid sister, and boring Aunt Zelda, into a team for the next two days, ready for the championship playoff. And it will give the bride's parents the satisfaction that your family is covering a share of the expenses. Because the grooms's family usually hosts, and pays for, the rehearsal dinner.

Let's think about this for a moment. The next day, you are going to be one of the co-stars of the equivalent of a major Hollywood production. (Along with your bride and the Dress.) So why do you have to put on a party before the party?

*Sherri and James both had parents who were divorced and remarried. On Sherri's side of the family, her two sets of parents got along quite well, and were, in fact, rather good friends, as were all the grown children that second marriages collect.*

*James' family was another matter. His parents had divorced so that his father could marry his mother's best friend. (If this sounds like a Hollywood script, it isn't. These are all true stories, I promise.)*

*This formal wedding would be the first time James' mother and stepmother had seen each other since THE DISASTER. Sherri and James were understandably nervous.*

*James' mother held the rehearsal dinner at her small house, inviting the entire bridal party of ten people, all the parents and all of their children and families. The food was a buffet dinner, with guests balancing plates on their laps if they were lucky enough to find a seat.*

*The last ring of the doorbell was the dreaded arrival of James' father and his wife. No one even heard the chimes at first, because the house was so full of people, packed together, laughing and talking and getting reacquainted.*

*James' mother and stepmother couldn't stay unfriendly*

*in such a close crowd. Soon, they were refilling the buffet table together and chatting just like the old friends they were.*

What a different scene that meeting would have been if the two women had first met in the church foyer, all dressed up, nervous and stiff, organ playing just before the ceremony, separated by formality.

All right, you're saying, my bride and I have known each other all our lives, so have our families. Why do we need another party?

Well, you really do need a rehearsal, and then everyone has to eat somewhere. Trust me, you'll have fun.

If you have a mother who loves to give parties, you may want to turn this whole chapter and the planning over to her, or you and your bride may decide to host the event yourself. Either way, we'll break the party down into planning stages.

### WHO WILL BE THE HOSTS?

As I said before, the groom's family usually takes this responsibility, especially if the bride's side is paying for most of the rest of the wedding.

However, sometimes the two families will decide to split all the expenses evenly, or sometimes the bride and groom have chosen to pay for parts or all of the wedding by themselves. Make this decision when you are laying out the budget for the entire event.

For this chapter, we will assume that the groom and his parents are hosting and paying for the party.

## WHEN DO WE START PLANNING?

Wait until you and your bride have settled into the plans for the wedding itself. Of course, you have to know the ceremony date, place, style, before worrying about the rehearsal.

Your bride will have so many details on her mind, she probably won't even want to discuss the rehearsal and dinner until she has settled other important choices, like the color of icing on her cake or the style of the bridesmaids shoes. (These really are major concerns to the people involved.)

Somewhere in this madness, decide with your parents (and the bride, of course), what kind of party you want. A formal dinner in a restaurant might have to be booked well in advance.

## WHAT KIND OF PARTY SHOULD WE HAVE?

This is not meant to be a second extravaganza, just a fun gathering of those in the wedding party. It is a chance to showcase your family's interests and talents.

*Chris and his father and two brothers specialized in barbershop quartet. Before the food was served, they serenaded the guests and Stefanie, the bride, with a series of progressively cornier songs. They ended with a popular song, cleverly rewritten to include the names and personalities of both families.*

Can't sing or dance? Let the location be the star.

*Carolyn's family was from the Midwest, and most of them had never been to California. She and Nick took their party to the beach, hosting a picnic on a warm summer evening. By sunset, the two families were good friends, and the visitors had a wonderful memory to take back to Kansas.*

Most rehearsal dinners take place in a restaurant or the groom's parents' home. Obviously, the final decision rests with whoever must pay the bill.

## WHO IS INVITED?

Everyone attending the rehearsal should be included, usually excluding only service personnel like the organist, although you might want to include this person also, if she is a friend, or good acquaintance from your church.

DON'T FORGET TO INCLUDE THE MINISTER, AND HIS WIFE, AND THE WEDDING COORDINATOR. This is just a case of good manners. They may politely decline, or may actually attend the dinner, but should always be invited.

All of the wedding party will attend — bridesmaids, and groomsmen with their spouses or dates, ring-bearer and flower girl with their parents, and both the bride's and your parents, grandparents, and brothers and sisters with any spouses or significant others. If there are any visitors from a long distance away, you might want to include them, as well as any aunts and uncles or godparents.

Yes, I know, the guest list is growing, just like it did for your wedding. Hopefully, we have now included those people you are closest to and kept the group small enough to really enjoy.

Invitations are usually sent out soon after the wedding invitation itself. These don't have to be as formal, and, in fact, should give the guests a clue about the type of party they can expect. You don't want your grandmother arriving for a beach picnic in her best Sunday dress.

## WHAT HAPPENS AT THE PARTY?

To look at a typical rehearsal dinner, we will take the most normal scenario. You have a rehearsal of your ceremony at your church on Thursday or Friday night for a Saturday wedding.

Your bride will be wearing a dress or dressy pant outfit, probably white. She will be nervous and possibly grumpy. This is not because she is marrying you, but because she still can't find the right color nail polish, and one bridesmaid's dress isn't finished. If you want to get a huge number of Romance points here and put her mind back on track, surprise her with a corsage, single rose, or tiny bouquet to carry for the rehearsal.

Both mothers have given a good deal of thought to their own outfits too, and both are also overwhelmed with details to be handled. Compliments on their appearance or even a kiss on the cheek are good here.

You will be wearing an outfit to match your bride's in formality. (Remember, I didn't promise you those jeans.) If you're not sure what to wear, ask the bride, or even your mother, if she's the hostess.

Once the rehearsal is finished, everyone heads for the restaurant. *Sean and Allison wanted to be sure that the two sets of relatives got acquainted. Instead of the usual U-shaped large table, guests sat at small tables for four or six, all placed close enough together for easy conversation. Sean and his father directed everyone to their seats, making sure to mix up the families, so that new people got to meet each other.* This works for some groups, but not others. The main point here is that you may want to plan the seating arrangements ahead of time, if only to be sure that everyone has a place to sit to balance a buffet plate.

A short program, before or after the meal, helps focus everyone's attention. You and your bride might make a toast or speech, you both can thank your parents for their love and support, tell the group about your feelings for each other, or reminisce about the past with various relatives or members of the wedding party.

*Michael and Trisha had a quick story to tell about each of their attendants, which they told as they handed out their gifts to the wedding party - a thoughtfully different one to each person, chosen to be personal and relate to the story being told.*

This last story brings up the subject of gifts. You should plan on a thank you present to each of your groomsmen, who have spent both time and probably money to stand by your side. Your bride will do the same with each of her girls.

These don't have to be expensive gifts, and they don't have to be the same for all the men. Typical items are a nice pen, men's jewelry, a special CD, pocket knives, good sunglasses. You can have them gift wrapped, or ceremoniously present each one in front of the guests.

Other people may make toasts or short speeches, particularly your parents, who are hosting the party. Some families like to include a prayer for the bride and groom.

A short video or slide show about the two of you can be fun, if you aren't planning to have one at the reception.

This is also the time for any entertainment by family members or friends. Just remember this is not meant to be a full concert - everyone needs a good night's rest.

When it's time to leave, don't forget to thank your parents for the party, and say good night to your almost-in-laws. Tell your bride you love her, kiss her good night, and try to get some sleep yourself.

# The Wedding Day

## Chapter 11

Finally, although it seemed like preparations would go on forever, The Big Day has arrived.

Countless books advise your bride to spend the wedding-day morning doing wonderful things like taking a leisurely bubble bath. What she actually does is frantically take care of last minute crises, from broken nails to no flower delivery.

This is probably why tradition still says that the bride and groom don't see each other before the ceremony. It's not bad luck in general, it's short tempers due to stress that cause trouble, and I have seen it cause pre-ceremony fights between two otherwise loving and calm people.

*Carol and Bill are both professional people who carefully organized their wedding with the efficiency of a well run ship, including plans to take all of the posed photographs before the ceremony.*

*Carol's photographs were first, and she and her bridesmaids were amazingly punctual.*

*Then it was time for Bill to arrive at 1:00. No one came. At 1:15, someone called Bill's house to be told that he had just started to dress. At 1:30, no Bill. At 1:45 he arrived, annoyed because everyone had been calling to rush him.*

*Here stood Carol, looking like a princess, beside a beautiful lake complete with swans. What were her first words of love to her future husband? "YOU'RE LATE!"*

Yes, there was a wedding and yes, they are still happily married.

So what do you do all day? Let's look at a make-believe ideal wedding day from the groom's point of view. There is often a long distance between dreams and reality, so the best wish I can give you for your Day is that your reality comes close to our ideal.

Let's pretend that your ceremony will take place at 5:00 at your church. If your wedding is early in the morning, you will obviously have to readjust this schedule and eliminate some things.

# MORNING

You probably attended the rehearsal dinner the previous night. (Not the bachelor party, which was held several days or a week before.) So sleep as late as you can and, when you get up, eat breakfast. At the risk of sounding like your mother, food is very important. I have seen several brides, grooms, and countless ushers keel over during the ceremony from lack of sleep and too much partying coupled with no food all day long.

After breakfast, you might want to check in with the best man to see if everything is running smoothly, including the ushers and their tuxedos.

A call to your parents is also a nice idea. The groom's parents don't have much to do until the ceremony and, since they are, in a way, responsible for you being there, giving them some attention is thoughtful.

The rest of the morning can be spent any way you choose. Wisdom suggests that you don't try to play eighteen holes of golf at a course across town, or engage in any sport where you can get easily injured.

*Don innocently drove across town on the morning of his wedding to get his hair trimmed by his favorite barber, and had planned to drive from there directly to the church.*

*What he didn't realize was that a tornado the night before had played havoc with the streets he would normally have traveled back to the church. He became entangled in a major traffic jam caused by downed trees, repair trucks and onlookers viewing the destroyed homes. The wedding started forty-five minutes late.*

Playing your favorite sport can be relaxing, but also risky. *Allen decided to go scuba diving with friends and wore a borrowed face mask. Because of improper fit, it suctioned to his face underwater, and all of his wedding photos showed a red circle around a bright red eyeball.*

Whatever you do, sports or visiting with friends, don't forget to eat lunch.

By 1:00, it is time to start getting dressed. Give yourself a total of one hour to shower, shave and put on your tux. This time may be all at your home, or partly at the church, if you are dressing there. I usually suggest that everyone gets dressed at home. That way you will not forget your socks or something else important.

Before leaving your house, you will go over the checklist you have made of everything you should take to the church - rings, marriage license, wallet, watch, car keys, card or present for bride, glasses, etc.

# ARRIVAL AT THE CHURCH

Unless you live around the corner from the church, allow an hour to get there. One good traffic jam can ruin months of planning, so leave your house between 2:30 and 3:00.

Why get to the church so early? Photographs! The photographer will want you, your family and your groomsmen all dressed, boutonnieres in place, ready for pictures by at least 4:00, possibly earlier. Of course, you have already checked this time with the photographer.

If there is a coordinator at your church, you will first check in with her and make sure everything is in order.

If the bride arrives at any point while you are in front of the church, go quickly to wherever you are directed so that she may enter without being seen by you. You get no Romance points for spoiling the bride's first appearance to you in the way she has always imagined.

As your family and groomsmen arrive, you greet them and then help the best man keep this group together and attentive to the photographer. This is a person who will be with you all day, and you will develop a love-hate relationship. You want good pictures but you also want to be left alone. Accomplish both by quick cooperation during the posed sessions and you shouldn't be bothered too much.

By the time these photos are finished, your minister has arrived. It is time for you and the best man to disappear from public view, possibly into the minister's office or wherever else you are directed, and say a few words to the minister. Then, hopefully, you will have a few quiet minutes with your best man and possibly your parents.

Check the location of the rings and license, and make sure your gift or card has been delivered to the bride.

# CEREMONY

Now the minister comes to get you. Organ music is playing, and it is time to follow the minister and best man into the church. You are terribly nervous and try to put a pleasant expression on your face. If it helps, remember that as soon as the first bridesmaid starts down the aisle, all eyes will be on the girls.

The organist plays several loud chords, everyone stands and your bride comes floating down the aisle, someone in a white dress and veil, her hair in an arrangement you have never seen before.

You unfreeze your feet from the floor and step forward. You shake hands with her father, take her arm, and the two of you advance toward the minister. When you stop, you tell her how wonderful she looks, even if you have no idea at this instant whether or not this is the right bride.

The ceremony progresses at an endlessly slow and amazingly fast pace. You do all of the rituals, standing next to your bride without locking your knees tight, which can be one of the first steps towards a faint.

At the end of the ceremony, you put her veil back, using both hands to gently lift the veil up and over her hairdo and headpiece (see Chapter 5, The Veil) and give her a romantic kiss, length of your choosing, but not a quick peck or an attempt to match the Guinness record for time. The organ music begins, and you turn to the audience. You take your wife's (yes, wife's) arm and start up the aisle. If you two have planned this, you stop to greet the parents and grandparents. The walk out of the church should not be too hurried (you will run over the photographer) or too slow. Try not to look stunned.

Another kiss for the bride is always a good idea as you exit the church doorway. But keep moving - there is a line of attendants also exiting, potentially waiting to start a gigantic doorway pileup if you aren't careful.

Everyone wants to kiss and hug, and the pesky coordinator is trying to lead the group around to the side to sign the license and take photos while the guests leave their seats.

Follow her advice, keep moving, and do your hugs when she tells you to stop moving. Otherwise, all of the guests and the wedding party get into a tangle which can take a half-hour to an hour to resolve, leaving some guests sitting idly at the reception and some waiting forever in front of the church to greet you after your photos. I know it's a pain, but that's what it's like when you're a star.

Signing the license is a simple procedure. Usually just the best man and maid-of-honor actually do it, while you and your bride watch. The best man will quietly hand the appropriate envelope to the minister. Next step is the formal photos. These can be taken in the church, a garden, a park, or at the reception. Let's say they are taken at the church. You have previously alerted the wedding party and family members to be present, not in the parking lot decorating cars. Looking for one brother-in-law to complete the family photo can ruin your time schedule.

Everyone is still very excited at this point, and probably talking loudly. Remember, you are still in a place of worship and should act accordingly.

When pictures are finished, it's time to leave the church. The best man will go out first. Guests are going to throw rice, and he will alert them to be ready. He will make sure the bridal car (or carriage or boat) is ready. If you have planned for a bottle of champagne in your limousine, the best man will check to be sure it is in place.

You have the train problem under control, and the two of you leave the church to the applause of your friends. You approach the car, someone opens the door and here we are, dress problems again. A skirt appropriate for a medieval carriage has to be crammed through a modern car doorway. Be helpful, principally by holding the door or her hand for balance as she enters, and let the bridesmaid deal with all of that skirt. Once your bride is safely seated, go around to the other door and enter the car, rather than make her scoot across the seat.

Now, relax. It is your first, and probably last time for the day, to have a few moments alone with your wife. Be as Romantic as you want. Kiss, hug, laugh, snuggle, joke — just remember, someone else is present, driving the car!

# RECEPTION

Whether your reception is at the church, a home, a hotel or a restaurant, the activities usually follow a fairly standard format. For this make-believe day, we will have a reception in the ballroom of a local hotel.

When you arrive at the hotel, exiting the car will cause the same problems as entering, only in reverse. I will not belabor this point any more, since by now you have graduated to expert in train handling.

You will probably be met at the hotel by the manager for your reception, or the band leader or disc jockey; whoever is going to be in charge of the coordination. If not, send your best man to find this person, to prepare for your entrance.

The bridal party may enter to fanfare and applause, or it may form a receiving line to greet the guests as they enter.

Following your entrance are a number of activities throughout the party. They may occur in any variety of sequences, and should be planned well ahead by you, your bride, the parents and the coordinator to avoid confusion and misunderstanding. We will look at each event from the groom's point of view, in a somewhat logical order of progression.

# FIRST DANCE

This may occur as soon as you enter, or after the meal is finished. Technically, no one else is supposed to dance until after you and the bride, so take this into consideration in your planning.

This is not the time to learn the Viennese waltz. You and your bride have chosen the song long before now, informed the musicians, and have danced to it before. If you two have spent months taking dancing lessons, now is the moment to show off.

If you haven't, now is not the time to tell her that you hate to dance. Be prepared, even if your ability is limited. Almost every bride's daydreams include gliding around the dance floor with her own Prince Charming. Don't let her down. Some practice, ahead of time, and a few loving words during your dance will reap huge benefits on this day and in the years ahead.

Remember, we're dealing with Romance. Even if your most graceful dance step is a side-to-side two-step, do it with panache and love, and you will have wet eyes all around the room, including your bride's. That's the idea.

After your dance together, it is traditional to dance with the parents for the second dance. Various etiquette books suggest various sequences. Sometimes both sets of parents will come onto the dance floor, dance with their spouses, then change with the bride and groom in a variety of combinations. Sometimes, the bride and groom will go into the audience and bring the parents out to dance with them. Whatever combination you choose should be well planned ahead of time.

The entire wedding party dances during the third song, and then the other guests join in.

# TOAST

The first toast is given by the best man (See Chapter 3). During the toast, all guests will raise their glasses; all except you and your bride. You do not raise them, even if you are standing up and therefore holding them, because you are the ones being toasted. As the toast words are spoken and the guests lift their glasses higher, you and the bride may raise your glasses to each other and drink.

If you are going to do the crossed-arms toast, this can be a little tricky. You both need to hold your glass in the right hand (or both use the left) in order for this to work. You cross arms and you each drink from your OWN glass, while looking into each other's eyes. Remember, particularly if you are both standing, she is probably shorter than you and it is very hard for her to take a sip if her hand is at your lip level, four inches above her head. Sip gently - neither of you wants liquid down the front of your clothing.

Other people may also give toasts. The fathers, ushers,

relatives or friends. Traditionally this was a male job, but not any more and often mothers or bridesmaids will also offer toasts. If you wish to speak, now is a good time.

Of course, you have given thought to this speech before now. All that the guests may have heard you say is "I do" - appropriate but not any indication of your personality or intellect. Take your time, try to relax, and don't forget to smile.

You thank the brides' parents for the wonderful wedding and for their daughter; thank your parents for raising you; thank your wedding party for their help and the guests, in general, for coming. You may tell short and tactful stories of how you met, your future plans, etc. A good ending is always to toast your new wife.

## DINING

During your meal, there will be a constant flow of activity. Friends will be coming up to talk to you, the coordinator will be checking details with you, the photographer is buzzing around, and your new father-in-law is determined to introduce his best friend. Just be sure that both you and your bride take some time to sit down and eat. Many couples have no idea what food was served at their wedding and leave for their honeymoon tired and hungry.

## CAKE-CUTTING

Here comes that photographer again, to tell you what to do. In this case, listen up. How many cakes have you cut?

A good photographer, or the reception coordinator, will show the two of you how to pose so that the guests can see you, the pictures will be good, and you can do the job properly.

On the actual first slice, the bride usually guides the knife while the groom has one hand under hers on the knife handle and the other hand around her waist.

Should you smash the cake in her face? Only your conscience can answer. The crowd may love it, but your bride may never forgive you for ruining her perfect makeup. It may be totally inappropriate for your type of guests, or the twinkle in your bride's eye may warn of her impending sneaky smash. Good luck.

## THROWING THE BOUQUET

This is totally handled by the Master of Ceremonies - band leader, D.J., etc., and the girls. You get to watch all those sweet bridesmaids turn into vicious animals and back in ten seconds.

## THROWING THE GARTER

If your family and friends, or the brides, are quiet and reserved, that's the way this event will also be. However, this is usually one of the rowdiest parts of the reception.

The announcer will call for all of the single men. If there are some that you know aren't coming forward, go to the microphone and give their names to the announcer, or call them up yourself. Be merciless, up to a point.

The bride will then step forward and, usually, be seated in a chair. This is to keep her from falling over while balancing on one foot in a high heel.

The single men are grouped behind her chair, so that the guests and that photographer can see the action.

The band will start to play, usually something like "The

Stripper", and the men will start all sorts of whistling and shouting.

You kneel on one knee to remove the garter, remembering that for your guests and for the photographs, your rear is probably not your best angle.

Hands, teeth, whatever can be used to remove the garter, in a sedate or sexy fashion. Let your taste be governed by your crowd.

Don't throw the garter too quickly. Help your bride up, and out of the way. Be sure the chair is removed. You don't want a male guest to have a broken nose that he got from falling over that chair in the melee.

Now, wait for a count from the announcer, usually "One, two, three". He should try to build the suspense first, so give him time.

Before turning your back to the men for the throw, take a brief look at where they are to judge for distance and height. Look up for overhead obstructions. A low ceiling will make a high-thrown garter land back at your feet quickly, with twenty guys on top of you. And most chandeliers don't need the extra decoration of a garter stuck in them.

On the count of three, throw backwards over your shoulder, then turn to watch the mayhem you have created.

# LEAVING THE RECEPTION

You and your bride may stay at the reception until the very end, savoring every minute, or you may be leaving at a prearranged time to catch a plane.

By now you have been photographed, hugged, kissed and congratulated for hours, your smile is frozen in place and you just want peace and quiet. Almost! Just a few more things to do.

If you have any responsibility for paying the bill, alert the necessary person to prepare it.

Tell your best man you are getting ready to go, so that he can organize transportation, clothing, or any other jobs he may have.

Alert the D.J. or Master of Ceremonies.

If you are changing clothes, you will usually do this separately from the bride.

This next part is rather important, and is best illustrated with a true story. It sums up the philosophy I have tried to develop throughout this book. That is, know the basics, plan ahead, and have lots of time for Romance and emotion, done with your own unique style. That's what this special day is all about.

### One Final Story

*Doug and Ann had a beautiful reception held at the bride's parents' home. They had already changed into their traveling clothes and were standing just inside the front door.*

*Outside, most of the guests had gathered to throw rice as the couple came out to their car.*

*Inside, Ann was hugging people good-by, including both sets of parents and family members, when Doug held up his hand to silence the group. He made a short speech, addressed to the bride's parents, which went something like this: "I have already thanked both families for everything they have done for us, to make this day so wonderful but I have one more thing to say." He turned to Ann's parents, who were holding hands. "When we leave this house, I know I am taking with me one of your most precious possessions - your daughter. You have nurtured her and loved her and helped her become the beautiful woman I love.*

*"This is a great treasure and I thank you for it. I just hope that our home will be filled with the laughter and love I see around me right now."*

*Of course, that brought down the house, and there was not a dry eye in sight. Then, amid hugs and kisses and more tears, the bride and groom ran through a shower of rice and drove away to live happily ever after.*

Your bride and I thank you for the time and caring you took to read through all of this.

My wish for you is the same as that for all of the couples I have watched throughout their wedding day. May your wedding be joyous and wonderful, and be the perfect beginning of your life together.